How Water of Life Was Built

a gift to me from my sweet and dear friends Dee Holman, her daughter Natalie + her children

Jan 2016

How Water of Life Was Built

DAN CARROLL

WITH **REBECCA ENGLISH**

For more information e-mail Water of Life Community Church at
info@wateroflifecc.org

Published by Water of Life Community Church
Fontana, California, U.S.A.
www.wateroflifecc.org
Printed in the U.S.A.

Library of Congress Control Number: 2010941415
ISBN-13: 978-0-9913138-4-6
ISBN-10: 0-9913138-4-6

Cover design by Danny Blanton
Interior design by InsideOut CreativeArts
Additional editing by Steven Lawson

Contents

Dedication

*This little historical book is dedicated to my family—
the ones who made this history happen.*

To Shane and Katie, My Children

You paid the deep price for Water of Life Community Church to become what it is today. I remember all those untold stories that we shared during those difficult early years, from setting up chairs in the childcare center every Saturday night to the times I was gone serving somebody else's family when you wanted me home.

I often prayed for both of you that you wouldn't grow discouraged or walk away from Jesus when things were difficult—and you didn't! Not only did you not walk away, but you both ran to Jesus and fell deeply in love with Him. You both stood with me and helped me. You never wavered when people took advantage of you being preacher's kids or told you how to live, act, and dress—even when it drove you nuts.

You have both, at one time or another, been employed by Water of Life and served there faithfully and admirably. So this story is yours as much as it is mine. I love you more than you will ever know, and today I am so happy to be known as your father!

To Gale, My Wife

Words fail to describe you, my wife and my friend. You are more than a conqueror in Christ. You are the dearest of them all, such a servant and lover of Jesus and others. You have always been there for me; whether you agreed with a situation or totally disagreed, you have stood with me. When you were troubled and uncertain, you stood with me. When I failed, you encouraged me. I never had a clue that God would work it all out for us like He has, but I am so grateful that you said yes to spend your life on me thirty-seven years ago. It has been a wild ride, and you have made it all worth it! Thank you for making the destiny that Jesus had for both of us possible by living out your faith every day.

Preface

I have been the pastor of six or seven churches—all named Water of Life Community Church. That's right, Water of Life has grown so much throughout the years that it really has been a different church at each stage.

There was the small Bible study, then the church plant in a rented childcare center (whew, the smells that went along with that). We grew a little and moved into a business park. That worked for a while, but really only a short time. So we went into our rent-a-school stage—at Ruth Musser and at Vineyard. We grew from fifty to one hundred to several hundred. Each time we moved, we had to stretch and change and meet new needs.

When we reached one thousand in attendance, we simply had to get our own facility. Sounds easy, right? Ah, the drama, speed bumps, and miracles that came with our move to and growth on East Avenue in Fontana. We learned how to perpetually walk in faith!

At East Avenue we have built a worship center, a chapel, venues, and parking lots—things I had never dreamed of when I was pastor of the first little Water of Life. We have opened offsite venues in Upland and Rancho Cucamonga and rented Glen Helen Regional Park for special events. Sometimes I ask, "How did this all happen, God? I just wanted to be a missionary!"

This little book tells the stories of these six or seven Water of Life churches. The journey has been a wild ride, and it is recounted as best as I can remember—with some help from my long, long-time assistant, Susan DePaola, my numbers guy, Mark Bluethman, my wife, Gale, and my editors, Rebecca English and Steven Lawson. We pored over my teaching and the stories I have told throughout the years and picked out some of the highlights—including our million-dollar miracle and the time I almost quit!

At every Water of Life Church I have pastored, it seems as if we have always been building. That's because we have! This book is full of details about our buildings, yes. But from the outset let's get it right—we have built not to have a big church or an impressive worship center but so that we could serve people—the people God has brought to us, the people God has made part of Water of Life. We like to say that we have a passion for God and a compassion for people. That really sums up who we have been from the beginning and who we still are today.

I tell the story from my perspective, as I have lived out this wild adventure. But our story of faith isn't just my story. This is also the story of thousands and thousands of people who have come through our doors and who call Water of Life home.

As I tell the story, I think of so many of those people. There is Rolo Santos, who has been with me from the beginning. Jim and Denise Shenton—it all started in your living room!

Along the way others have come. I am going to get the chronology wrong, but here goes: Kevin and Sheila Bolka, Scott and Ruth-Ann Taylor, Bob Erickson, Jeff Krausman, Kenny and Penny King, Jack and Dolly Carnine, Pam Havlick, Rebecca Gadberry, Denny and Carolyn Barlett, Rose and Randy Geary, Peter and Cheryl Felsch—you sacrificed to birth this church. Brian and Melody Snowball, Mark and Cindy Bluethman, Nico and Diane Mendez, Chuck and Barb Belk—how could we have grown Water of Life without your faith?

God has brought along Paul and Susan DePaola, Jeff Keller, Joyce Carlsen, Vicky Anderson, Sal Angulo, Rob Hopper, Willie and Anna Ulibarri, Arden Schlect, Matt France, Julianne Smith, Mark and Susan Nuaimi, and Andy Taylor, who grew up in the church and stayed to lead our worship team.

I like talking with people, but I cannot possibly pastor everyone. That's why this is also the story of Glen Totten, Bob Bryant, and Linda Jones. You guys make it happen!

I am humbled as I list the names. Each person here has his or her own story of faith that could have been added to this little book, and so do others—so many others. I know, I have left out many names. If you have been part of Water of Life—from driving a shuttle to editing a video to singing on the worship team to distributing food at CityLink to a thousand other contributions—know that this is your story too. And I thank you.

I put together this book to celebrate all that God has done as we move into another chapter as a church. It will be released the weekend that we move into our new worship center, on November 14–15, 2015. I invite you to read about and enjoy the history of Water of Life and to look forward with me to what God will do next. It looks as if I am about to become the pastor of a new church, and this one will be called Water of Life too!

On July 11, 1997, I wrote a Scripture quote in my journal: "Wait patiently on Me, and I will do it" (Ps. 37:5, 7). A few days later, a woman in our church gave me this wooden wishing well with a Water of Life sign on it. Somebody had written a Bible verse and taped it on the well's bucket. It was Psalm 37:7. This little gift provided one of many amazing words that we have been given from God over the years. To this day I display it in my office.

RELUCTANT PASTOR

1982–1990

Twenty-five years ago. Wow. That is an impossibly long time ago, yet in many ways it seems like just yesterday.

That's when we started this adventure called Water of Life Community Church. "We" would be Pastor Rolo, my wife Gale, my two kids, a handful of dear friends, and me. Water of Life was at first what you would call very small.

Pastor Rolo actually lived with my family back then. For his part in helping plant the church, we paid him really well: he got free rent and boxes of cereal! Yes, that is correct, cereal. Whatever brand was on sale or my wife had coupons for, that's what he ate. It was a good deal—not for him but for us.

God was smiling upon us when He sent us a man like Pastor Rolo—someone who would work for food and not grumble. Amazing. This not-so-ordinary approach pretty much says it all. Ours was a simple beginning but quite a miraculous one. It was just God and us, but mostly God.

You see, when it came to the launch of Water of Life, God made something out of nothing. We worshiped without a worship team, fellowshipped without a church building, launched a ministry without office space, and had a pastor who instead wanted to be a missionary—yep, that was me.

I had never dreamed of becoming a senior pastor, and for many years starting a church was the last thing on my mind. After college I had worked as a high-school basketball coach and a teacher. Sports had been my life! I had even dragged my family to upstate Idaho for a brief season—there I'd had a really good basketball team and a really bad ending. (I'll save my crazy Idaho saga for another time.)

By 1982 my career as a basketball coach was over, and I had landed back in Southern California in somewhat of a mess. For a few years I was a youth pastor, then a part-time substitute teacher. But what I really wanted most was to go into missions—preferably in a country far, far away. (Mind you, this was my idea, not my bride's. She loved God, but living overseas was the last thing on her mind!)

I could dream about big adventures all I wanted, but what Gale and I needed most in the years after we arrived back in California was for our marriage to be mended. During that season we were in the midst of a terribly painful journey. Our relationship was toxic. That's right; we had made mistakes—well, mostly I had made mistakes in my attitude toward her. But we were determined to stay in and get things restored.

Thankfully, Jesus knew exactly how to restore us. We went through lots of counseling. Spent lots of time in prayer. Had a few breakthroughs. And there were my basketball buddies.

In the late eighties Jesus connected me with a group of men who sustained me. I guess we really sustained each other, because most of them were hurting too. Every Tuesday night we gathered in the backyard at Jim Shenton's house in Upland, and we played hoops. Pastor Rolo was one of these guys, but he wasn't a pastor yet either. He was just Rolo Santos, a dear friend.

It's hard to have hope for the future when the agony of daily living is so great. At times during those days my pain over my marriage issues seemed unbearable. That's when Jesus did for me what He has done for so many others who turn to Him in times of crisis. He strengthened me with grace and love and friends. What Jesus did for me was supernatural, yet it also flowed through all those who He gathered around me. These men and our Tuesdays together became my lifeblood.

Each week, after we had played ball for a couple of hours, we gathered in the Shentons' family room. Soon enough the guys asked me to lead them in a Bible study.

At first I hesitated. How could I teach anyone about God at a time when my own marriage was so broken? Besides, I was going to be a missionary, wasn't I? I didn't want to get tied to ministry at home too tightly. My excuses didn't stop Jesus. Just as He does so often, as I taught from His Word, He showed up in spite of me.

After the guys and I studied God's Word each week, we would talk. My basketball buddies and I hurt so much that all our issues just tumbled out. We were amazingly transparent. No one ever attempted to hide weaknesses, and no one acted hyper-spiritual. We were just needy and hungry for God's presence.

Every time we met we were drenched with love from the Father's heart. The Holy Spirit graciously showed up, time after time. Amazingly, one of the guys He touched and healed the most was me, the Bible study teacher. That's how our Tuesdays went for about a year—basketball, Bible study, a lot of tears, a lot of deep healing.

God was sustaining and growing Gale too. He brought along a group of women to minister to her, and He started speaking to her.

While we slowly healed, Gale and I decided to spend a week during the spring of 1989 fasting and crying out to Jesus for direction. On Friday of that week, I received a call from my sister-in-law. I hadn't spoken with her for a while, but I knew that she had given her life to Jesus in the recent past. God was moving in her and in my brother in fresh and powerful ways.

My sister-in-law told me that Jesus had clearly spoken to her that day during a class that she was attending in Hawaii. She was on the campus of University of the Nations, a missionary training school hosted by Youth With A Mission (YWAM). She said that God had told her that I was supposed to come to that school, and she added that she and my brother were supposed to pay for the trip.

I wanted to be a missionary, yes. But I wasn't tempted by my sister-in-law's offer. With all that Gale and I were going through, flying off to some mission school that I had never heard of was not on my to-do list. And I knew that Gale would pass out over the idea. So I simply and politely said no.

I wanted to be a missionary, yes. But flying off to some mission school that I had never heard of was not on my to-do list.

But God rarely takes our "no" as a no. He is patient and persistent.

Two days after I talked with my sister-in-law, Gale and I went to the Vineyard Christian Fellowship in Anaheim, California, as we did every Sunday night in those days. During the service God showed up in quite an extraordinary way. He turned my "no" into a "yes."

As I remember it, the pastor had an altar call for people with sin in their lives. *Whew. That's not me this week*, I quickly and thankfully thought.

For the first time ever, Gale and I had been fasting and praying together. It had been one of the deepest and most intimate times with the Lord that we had ever experienced. So there was no need for me to go forward that night.

Then, in the midst of my reasoning, I clearly heard a voice—the one that I was growing to love deeply. Ever so softly the voice said, "Go forward, and go now." I clearly recall my stupid response: "No way. Some of the people here know me. I'm six feet eight inches tall—they'll all see me and think that I'm sinning. Some of them already think I'm clueless, and this will just confirm their suspicions."

All I heard was, "Obey Me now, and go forward."

I stood to my feet and started walking toward the altar, having no clue that God was about to alter my destiny. When I got to the front of the sanctuary, I had a remarkable feeling of being held in Jesus' hand. It was as if He had swooped in on me, wrapped me up, and was holding me.

As the worship team played and others prayed, I lifted my hands and began to surrender. I had never before lifted my hands in worship, though I had secretly longed to.

At that moment, God spoke to me again: "I am going to give you the desire of your heart."

I prayed, "Lord, I have spent the last two years laying all my desires down in order to save my marriage. Right now I have no idea what my desire is."

God continued, "I am going to send you to Hawaii so that you can touch nations."

I was starting to get it: "You mean that phone call Friday was You?"

"Yes, it was Me."

God had been speaking to and through my sister-in-law after all. But how on earth was I going to break this news to Gale? As I turned from the altar and made my way back down the aisle, I saw that Gale was watching me. Her look pointedly asked me, "What happened?"

I told her that I wasn't sure she wanted to know.

"I think I already know," she said. "We're going to Hawaii, aren't we?"

I almost fainted! "Are you kidding?" I asked. "How could you know that?"

"This morning when I was praying, the Lord told me that we were going."

Gale had never, ever wanted to go to the mission field, although I had asked her to join me overseas many times over the years. "You are really okay to go?" I asked.

I will never forget her answer.

"Sure, as long as it's Jesus who is taking me and not you."

Oh, my. That day we took our first steps into a wild world full of surprises and adventures.

Just a few months later, in August 1989, we boarded an airplane headed to Hawaii. Gale and I spent several months at the YWAM discipleship training school in Kona, Hawaii (which is part of University of the Nations), and then we traveled to Malaysia and Singapore, where we spent several more months as members of a short-term outreach team. While in Southeast Asia, I was even offered a job with a church.

We were with YWAM for about six months, and we really felt that we were going to permanently relocate to Malaysia. But upon our return to California, every door to the mission field kept closing, and everything pointed to us not going back overseas at that time. Gale and I were very troubled, but I was especially unhappy. If we weren't supposed to go overseas, what had this missionary training been all about?

My basketball buddies had continued meeting for Bible study while we were gone. Pastor Bob Erickson, who later was on our Water of Life staff, had led them in my absence. But the guys, including Bob, pressed me, "Will you please come back and lead us again?"

"Okay," I told them, "while Gale and I are waiting and trying to sort things out, I'll do it." The thing is, I went back to leading that study—and never got out of there!

After we'd met again for a while, the men's wives said, "The guys are really changing. Can we come too?" So we expanded to a couples' study on Friday nights and kept Tuesday nights for men only.

Shortly after picking the Bible study back up, in March 1990, God moved me to return to Malaysia for a second short-term outreach trip. Several of the guys in our Bible study group surprised me and asked if they could come along. This turned out to be another one of those wild adventures that Jesus led us into. Even though we weren't a church yet, you could say it was Water of Life's first missions trip!

After that trip to Malaysia, I kept playing basketball and teaching our small group at the Shentons' place. But Gale and I hoped and prayed to get to the mission field. As far as I was concerned, we couldn't get there quickly enough.

But that fall, one night after our Bible study, Pastor Rolo threw me a curveball.

He walked with me to the street, where I had parked my truck. When we reached the curb, he stopped me and showed me a cocoa can that had a slit in the top. Beside the slit was a note that read, "As the Lord leads, for Pastor Dan." Pastor Rolo handed me the cocoa can and said, "These people want you to be their pastor."

I looked at him like he was crazy. "I don't want to be their pastor."

He didn't back down. "I think you're supposed to plant a church."

"I think I'm supposed to go back to Malaysia," I said.

"Look," Pastor Rolo said, "let me tell you something. Those people in the meeting tonight put $1,600 in this can for you, and they're not getting a tax write-off for it."

He let that sink in a moment, then added, "They believe in what God is doing here, and they've put their money where their faith is, and that speaks. You need to obey God."

Now I'm way too big of a rebel. As soon as someone says the "obey" word, I think, *No*. This was not a happy day for me.

I told my wife about the can and the note, and we began to pray for direction—but I must admit that for me it was begrudging prayer. I wasn't eager to remain in Southern California, nor had I ever had a vision for planting a church there. In fact, so many of my friends had done exactly that and had failed. I had no desire whatsoever to attempt it.

I had been deeply touched during our time with YWAM. This latest turn didn't seem to fit at all—at least not as I saw it. But Jesus had a different view. He knew exactly what He was doing.

As it turned out, that conversation with Pastor Rolo was a supernatural moment. It didn't revolve around the money; it revolved around the confrontation. What spoke to my heart was the commitment of thirty-five people. I never even considered the money itself but only the people's hearts—that $1,600 spoke of their commitment, of their sacrifice. It blew me up and created a huge battle inside me.

Gale and I soon began to feel that the Lord was telling us to start a church right there in Rancho Cucamonga. Mind you, I was kicking and screaming all the way.

Faith is saying yes to God, even when everything in us screams no. It took me a while to figure out that it was better to obey God than to rebel, but when I finally did, everything changed. Just as I had obeyed and walked down the aisle at the Vineyard church service on that Sunday night, I now determined that I would obey God's voice again. And God was saying, *Just do this.*

So I agreed to start a church.

Secretly, though, I hoped that it would quickly fail.

SMALL BEGINNINGS

1990–1995

Once I said yes to starting a church, things moved fast. We needed a name. We asked everybody in our group to bring an idea to the next meeting, and we decided that we would draw lots. This all sounds very corny as I look back and remember, but our hearts were hungry for Jesus, and He was deeply in our midst. Lots or no lots, we were being led forward each step of the way supernaturally, and we were all keenly aware of it.

The following week we had eight different names on eight straws. We cut each straw a different length. Someone mixed them up and held them all, and we prayed over them: "Lord, we want Your name." Then we drew according to size, and the longest straw read "Water of Life." I added "Community Church," and that's how Water of Life Community Church was born.

Even though we were in the midst of birthing a church, I kept believing in the back of my mind that Gale and I were going overseas. I thought, *We'll obey, and then the Lord will close the church, and we'll go to the mission field.*

Touching nations was the desire of my heart, after all, and at the Anaheim Vineyard meeting God had told me that He would give me what I desired. In my mind our short-term missions trip had been a taste of the long-term fulfillment of God's promise to me. He surely would release me, and I could go to Malaysia soon, or so I thought. Over the years I have come to see that God always keeps His promises, but rarely do they work out as we anticipate that they will.

Now that we had a name, we needed a building. We couldn't keep meeting at the Shentons'. I began to snoop around the city. One afternoon I went over to the La Petite childcare center on the corner of Haven and Valencia. A nice lady greeted me, and I asked her about renting their space for our church. She laughed and said, "We've had three churches here in the last year, and they're all shut down, so I don't know if you really want to rent our building."

I said, "Yes, I do want to rent it!"

I thought, *The other churches all went under! This is a good thing for me.* I figured that renting La Petite would be a great exit strategy: the church wouldn't last, and Gale and I would be able to go to Malaysia while still having obeyed what God had asked us to do in starting a church in California.

So we borrowed fifty rusted folding chairs from the American Legion, Post 30, and on October 28, 1990, a group of twenty-one adults and eleven children gathered together to worship God at La Petite childcare center.

My wife and I had this little fiberglass trailer, about seven feet long, that we used for hauling camping gear when we went on vacation, which we kept parked by the side of our house. It was red and round, and the top lifted up. We always laughed at the thing because it looked like a ladybug. Every Saturday night we put our fifty borrowed chairs inside it, and we hooked it up to our Malibu station wagon. For those of you too young to remember, station wagons were the thing before minivans came along. We hauled this trailer down to La Petite every Saturday night, unloaded the chairs, and set up for Sunday services.

Our kids, Shane and Katie, hated this, because at La Petite we needed an oxygen mask. You know how it is in a little kids' preschool—those kids don't know where the toilet is, so the whole place smells. To deal with the odor, we went in with Lysol every week and sprayed everything. When people opened the door on Sunday morning, it was Lysol and urine. Whoa! It was the weirdest thing. The good news is that nobody ever fell asleep on me during church, because the ammonia level was so high.

Gale and I lived just a block north of La Petite, so my neighbors always saw us coming and going with our trailer. They joked, "What are you doing?" We would pull the trailer to La Petite, and they would drive by and see us. They would read our little signs out, "Water of Life Church," and would laugh, "Are you guys playing church?"

We knew that our neighbors were just giving us a hard time, but their ribbing stung. Stop and think about it. Having a church in a preschool isn't what I ever thought of as a life-fulfilling calling. La Petite is a long way from Kona or Kuala Lampur.

Sometimes it felt as if we *were* playing church. We didn't even have a worship team. We did have Jeff Krausman, though, and he always came with an armful of cassettes. When people asked what kind of music we had, I told them that our worship band was Jeff Krausman and the Cassettes.

Honestly, we did everything wrong that we possibly could do wrong, yet shockingly, we grew—slowly but surely.

I often asked God, "What are we doing?" It wasn't as clear back then, but we were just doing what God had told us to do. That's what faith is—simply obeying God, saying yes even when everything in us screams no. Doing what God tells us to do, one step at a time, is how we reach our destinies. It doesn't sound too romantic, but it does allow God to move in us with great authority and power.

We often don't grasp what God's up to. See, Hebrews 11:1 says, "Faith is the assurance of things hoped for, the conviction of things not seen." So faith is two things: it is in the future, and it is unseen.

When people can see things, everybody wants to be part of what's going on. But when the vision is in the future and unseen, people think we're crazy. A lot of us think that if God is in something, it's going to be easy to accomplish. No, no, no. Faith is about obstacles. Faith is about climbing the mountain with God. Faith is about pressing in when we want to give up.

How do we grow faith? Well, one way is just to stay in, say yes. Faith is putting the ladybug trailer on the Malibu station wagon and smelling the urine every Saturday night. It is staying in when the neighbors laugh. It is sticking with it, even when you think that you are supposed to be in Malaysia but you're in Southern California. Faith is about not giving up even when you want to quit. Faith is saying yes!

I couldn't see any hope or future in what we were doing, even though Pastor Rolo and the people who had been in the Bible study could. I did have hope for one thing, though: "God, I want to change people's lives someday. You have changed me so much—let me touch somebody else." That's what was unseen and hoped for in my heart. I didn't hope for a big church; I just had a passion for people.

So I stayed in.

The church met at La Petite for a year, and instead of closing down, we outgrew the place. In 1991 we moved to Vineyard Junior High School, also in Rancho Cucamonga. There we had room for Sunday services and one Sunday school class. Our church office was in Kenny and Penny King's home.

By January 1993, we had grown to 175 people, and we needed to move again. Another church contacted us about a building they knew about on Terra Vista Parkway, and that became Water of Life's next home.

As has become our DNA, there is a story behind our move to the new building. Some months before we moved, Gale and I were driving around Rancho Cucamonga one day when we noticed a new business park being built on Terra Vista Parkway, near Haven Avenue and just north of Foothill Boulevard. I casually turned to her and said, "If Water of Life Community Church could be anywhere in town, that's where I would want it to be."

A week later Gale was driving in the same area, and as she drove, she began to pray about the building. But as she approached the business park, she saw a sign—not a sign from God but a sign with another church's name on the building's façade.

He whispered something in Gale's ear that would change our lives: "They are building that for you."

Oh, boy, Dan is not going to be okay with this, she thought. And I wasn't.

It got worse. A few days later we received a mailer inviting us to the new church in town—theirs, not ours! I was discouraged. Water of Life didn't belong to a denomination. We had no financial backing or super rich supporters. We didn't even have printed flyers announcing our services. It was just us and God—but still mostly God.

Gale knew what to do. She prayed. And God reminded her that He knew what He was up to. When Gale asked Him about the Terra Vista site, He whispered something in her ear that would change our lives: "They are building that for you." She was aghast at the thought and didn't tell anyone—not even me.

Some months later I got a telephone call from someone at the Terra Vista Town Center church. The caller asked if we would be interested in taking over their lease, because they were closing their doors. Jesus had us right where He wanted us—totally dependent on Him as He unfolded His heart in our little church.

Now we had room! And the King family could have their home back, which we had rented the year before as our office.

Two and half years after we moved to Terra Vista, with attendance topping 750 people, we once again outgrew our facility. The decision was made to split the campus and relocate the adults five hundred yards up the street at Ruth Musser Middle School, while our children's and youth ministries continued to meet at the Terra Vista site.

As I write this account of our history some two decades later, I am struck by how simple the move sounds now—yet it was a time so full of struggle and excitement and day-to-day ministry. It is amazing how those early years were shaped by God. He brought the right people to help build Water of Life. Joyce Carlsen came to run the children's ministry. Glen Totten, Mark Bluethman, Nico Mendez, Chuck and Barb Belk, and so many others came along at just the right time. Many of them have now been with us for more than twenty years!

We showed love to people and prayed for them. We believed that God would heal marriages and mend broken hearts, and He did! Oh, how He did. One family after another walked into our church in desperate shape, and every time people came, God showed up to meet their needs.

All-night prayer meetings were a regular part of our journey. We gathered and cried out for God's presence, knowing that we had no idea what we were doing but that God knew exactly what He was doing. In spite of the inconvenience of having the children in one building and the adults a quarter mile up the street, we continued to grow deeper into God's heart as a people and larger as a church family.

It was during this time that Brian Snowball, a Native American guy, came to faith in Christ at our church. He was a great example of the healing work that God was giving us to do. Brian had recently been arrested on a DUI, and he was hungry for God to work in his life. One day he walked into our office and said, "How can I serve?" He had previously worked for Coors and had also been a thug who had collected money for a loan shark.

Brian started serving around our Terra Vista building—sweeping floors, wiping children's tables, doing little maintenance tasks. He was willing to do anything. In those days we never knew who was going to come in or what was going to happen, and to Brian it was all very exciting. Eventually he was put in charge of facilities, and he became a key figure in people's lives as he spoke to anyone he could about the love of God. He has been on our staff now for nearly twenty-five years. Today he is known as "Pastor Brian."

Brian was a great example of Luke 4:18–19, which became our call at Water of Life: "The Spirit of the Lord is on me, because he has anointed me to proclaim good news to the poor. He has sent me to proclaim freedom for the prisoners and recovery of sight for the blind, to set the oppressed free, to proclaim the year of the Lord's favor" (NIV). These verses define what Jesus was doing with our church and what He had called us to become. Ultimately they became the basis of our five core values: caring, healing, equipping, sending, and relationships (you can read more about them at the back of this book). This mission was born out of our passion for God and compassion for people.

God had clearly aborted my plan to move to Malaysia, but He had kept alive my hope to touch people's lives in that country and elsewhere. Shortly after we had started the church, in November 1990, I had planned another short-term outreach trip to Malaysia (my third trip there). A team of thirteen people from Water of Life, including Kevin Bolka and Jeff Krausman, came with me. That was the true beginning of our long-term relationship with churches and people in Malaysia. In 1992 we expanded to other countries, sending teams to Southeast Asia and to Mexico.

With these short-term missions trips, God kept His promise to fulfill the desire of my heart—and He did it on His terms. I had always loved the nations of the world, but now my desire took on new meaning, and it became the heart of God not only for me but also for the church to touch neighborhoods and nations. This was what Water of Life was going to be about.

So many times in those early years, my faith faltered. How often did I want to quit this church? Let me count. . . second thought, I'm not going to count. But each time I wanted to throw in the towel, I had faithful people around me who said, "No, we're not going to quit. God is in this, even if you're not. Just be quiet and stay in."

Michael Edwards was one of those people. Today he is a pastor of a church in Riverside and often a guest speaker at Water of Life. In the early days he was a neighbor of mine in Rancho Cucamonga. On many Saturday evenings, when I was ready to bail out, I would pound on his garage door, knowing that he was inside preparing for his Sunday service. Michael would let me in and motion for me to sit down in an area that he had turned into an office. We would pray together, and he would tell me why I needed to stay in. God in His wisdom and mercy gave me so many people like Michael. I cannot name everyone in such a short book, but without them I no doubt would have left.

God kept teaching me one small lesson at a time about how "faith is the assurance of things hoped for, the conviction of things unseen"—it is believing for what we can't see and for what is ahead of us. Faith believes for healing when other people don't. Faith believes for hope when other people don't have any. Faith believes that God will touch and change people when others don't think it can happen.

I just needed to yield to Jesus, saying yes over and over again. I was learning that without faith, it is impossible to please God.

FAITH FOR AN INHERITANCE

1995–1997

Water of Life quickly outgrew the tandem Terra Linda and Ruth Musser sites, just as we had our earlier locations. By 1995 we were jam packed and began to pray in earnest for a new church home.

Over the course of about a year, I personally visited every available property in the area. I exhausted every possibility, or so I thought, and found nothing that would work for us. After nine to ten months of searching, to come up empty was discouraging.

Around that time Dennis Larkin, a local pastor and a friend of mine, told me about Rancho Lindo Hospital on East Avenue in Fontana, just east of Rancho Cucamonga. The 74-bed facility, which had been operated by a British firm called Community Psychiatric Centers, was shutting its doors, and the property was for sale.

At that time East Avenue was basically out in the middle of nowhere. I wasn't sure that we really wanted to move out to the boondocks, but Peter Felsch and I called and left a message with the realtor. Peter, an Aussie I had met while in Malaysia with YWAM, was our administrator at the time and one of my best friends.

In the meantime, our families—the Carrolls and the Felsches—drove to the beach in San Clemente for a scheduled day away. While we were there, I received a phone call from the realtor. "Come on out," he said. "I'll show you the property." So we packed our gear and drove home early.

Peter and I went over to East Avenue believing for a miracle. We parked my truck by the curb and waited for the realtor. There wasn't a house in sight—just dirt fields and two buildings—one two stories high, the other a wide single story. I remember wondering if people would actually drive that far out to go to church.

We loved the property, but the buildings looked gigantic. We only had about a thousand people in the church at that time. We'd been looking at million-dollar places, mostly warehouses and old stores, and this place was huge, fully furnished with desks and chairs and conference tables, and being sold for $3.1 million. We were really taken by the place, but it was in a totally different category than what we'd been considering.

Peter and I sat at the curb by the two-story building and waited for the real estate agent for a long time—but he stood us up. Talk about stretching my faith. *Come on now!* I thought. *I was at the beach with my family. I drove all the way back from San Clemente just to meet this guy, and he doesn't show up!* Peter and I had gone there believing for a miracle, and we'd gotten nothing.

When Peter and I called the realtor the next day, he told us that the property had already been sold. The Guadalupe Home for Boys had grabbed it. This news was another setback. *Anything that's out there probably won't come our way*, I thought, discouraged. So we kept meeting at Terra Linda and at Ruth Musser Middle School. And we kept growing and looking.

Six months later, in February 1997, a lady in our church named Holly Moore handed me a little piece of paper. On it she had written me a note saying that while she had been praying about the building, God had put Psalm 37:9–11 on her heart for Water of Life—especially the word "inherit."

I get a lot of words from people. Many are not from God, but some of them are. The only way to know the difference is to pray. So I stuck that paper in my quiet-time Bible, and I prayed over it. But the message wouldn't go away. Holly's handwritten note just kept looking at me every morning, and I'd say, "Lord, what is it about this word?" I kept reading Psalm 37:7–9, especially verse 9: "Rest in the LORD and wait patiently for Him. . . . Those who wait for the LORD, they will inherit the land."

"Lord, what does that mean?" I prayed. "I've been waiting for two years. Moses waited in the wilderness for forty years—if I have to wait that long, I'll be in a rest home."

Finally I telephoned Holly and said, "Do you know what this means?"

She says, "Oh, yeah, the Lord told me what it means."

"What does it mean?"

"Somebody is going to give us an inheritance to buy property."

I thought that was a little funny. So I put the paper away and kept praying.

Three weeks later my phone rang. On the other end of the line was a woman named Helen Lovett. I had never met this lady, never even seen a picture of her. Helen said to me, "I want to tell you something. I'm dying of cancer, and I want to leave my estate to your church."

This is a true story.

All I said was, "All right." But I was thinking, *Hmmm, this is pretty interesting.*

"Hospice wants my estate, TBN wants my estate," Helen continued. "But people from your church are bringing cassette tapes to my house of your messages, and they're encouraging me and praying for me and bringing me communion while I'm dying, and the Lord has been really clear with me that I'm supposed to give my estate to your church."

Wow. The word from Holly Moore and Psalm 37:9 came to my mind. This was blowing me up.

At the same time, we needed to be really thoughtful and careful with this lady. We didn't want to look like a shark swimming around a sinking boat. "What do You want to do here, God?" I prayed.

On April 3, 1997, I called a lady in our church, Jane Barry, who was a CPA and did financial planning. I said, "Jane, would you please go see Helen Lovett tonight and talk to her about her estate? I don't want you to do anything. Be really thoughtful and kind, no pressure. Just listen to her."

Jane said, "Sure, Dan. I'll do that."

When I came home that night, the light on my voice recorder was flashing. I pushed the button and heard a message from Jane: "Pastor Dan, I went to Helen Lovett's house tonight," she reported. "Everything is done. I called the vice president of Vineyard Bank, and Helen signed over her CDs and her house. She signed over everything to us."

I called up Jane and said, "Thank you for listening to God and not your pastor."

"Everything is not supposed to be done, girl," I said out loud to myself. "I told you not to do that."

At the end of the voicemail, Jane said, "I know I wasn't supposed to do that, but I did. Bye!"

You know what I did? I picked up the phone, then I took a deep breath and started praying. "Okay, Lord, help me to be nice while I talk to Jane."

I called her. "Jane, this is Pastor Dan."

"Hi, Pastor Dan, how are you?"

"Not very good right now, because you didn't do what I asked you to do! I asked you to just go over, talk to the lady. What did you do? What happened, Jane?"

I was trying to be nice, but on the inside I was flipping out.

"Pastor Dan," Jane said, "I got there, and Helen started explaining everything. She told me that she's supposed to live for six more weeks, but while I was sitting there, the Lord told me to do it now."

"Oh, really? God told you to do it now? What did your pastor say, Jane?"

"I know. You said to not do it now. But Pastor Dan, I've been sitting under your teaching for years. You've always taught me to listen to the voice of God, and I heard it very clearly. God told me to do it now. So I did."

"Ohhh, okay."

What was I going to say to that? I'm the one who had taught her this. Now she'd done the right thing, and I didn't like it.

Two days later, on April 5, 1997, Helen Lovett died.

After hearing the news, I called up Jane and said, "Thank you for listening to God and not your pastor."

What if Jane had gone to visit Helen that night but hadn't been walking close to God? What if she hadn't been listening to the Holy Spirit's leading? Jane was strategically placed by God for the right purpose—for the miraculous to break forth in the situation.

Helen Lovett left Water of Life $250,000, enough for a down payment on a new property for our church.

Helen Lovett gave because she was eternally minded. She looked way ahead of herself, and she believed what other people couldn't believe, and she's now in heaven reaping all the benefits of everybody who has been and will be touched, healed, and saved at Water of Life. They are all going into her account. Is that amazing or what?

One Saturday afternoon not long after we had received Helen Lovett's inheritance, I was watching a football game on television. After the game Roy Rogers and Dale Evans came on the broadcast, talking about the East Avenue property that Peter Felsch and I had visited. They were strong supporters of Guadalupe Home for Boys, and they were explaining how the home couldn't get needed permits.

The home had actually bought the property before obtaining the permits. When nearby residents had found out that the home was going to house boys who had been criminals and that there would not be a fence around it, they protested. Hundreds of them had gone down to Fontana City Hall and stood against the Guadalupe Home. As a result, the city had denied the permit.

Later that day I drove over to East Avenue and looked at the property again. The two-story would be perfect as an office. The wide building could house the Sunday school. And there was enough empty space for a brand-new worship center. I could picture it all in place.

Could it be? I dared to think.

The $3.1 million price tag was still out of our league, not to mention that if we bought the land and the existing buildings, we would still need to build a sanctuary. We had never seen that kind of money at Water of Life.

As I surveyed the land and buildings that day, a million thoughts buzzed through my mind. Suddenly I found myself thinking about the International School of Theology (ISOT) at Arrowhead Springs in the nearby San Bernardino Mountains, which had been founded by Dr. Bill Bright of Campus Crusade for Christ.

I had graduated from ISOT's seminary and was close friends with the president at that time, Dr. Donald Weaver. I had heard from him that Campus Crusade was planning to move to Florida, where their new headquarters campus was located—but they wanted to leave the seminary on the West Coast. I wondered if ISOT would be open to buying the East Avenue site with us as a joint effort.

I didn't lose any time before meeting with the realtor. When I knew for sure that the property was back on the market, I called Dr. Weaver and asked him if he wanted to partner with us.

He was interested, but he needed to discuss it with the ISOT board of directors. Dr. Weaver arranged for the board to meet at and inspect the East Avenue property, and after four hours of discussions, the board accepted the plan.

We and ISOT agreed that the seminary would buy the two-story building and one acre of land for one million dollars. Water of Life would purchase the single-story building and the remaining thirteen acres. The seminary would also lease from us a wing of the single story, where they would house their fifty-five-thousand-volume seminary library.

In June 1997, we made our first joint offer on the property.

On July 13, we took 275 church members to East Avenue for a walk through. By faith we went into the courtyard and worshiped together. We asked God to give us the place. We didn't have the money to buy it, but we had the faith to try it.

Faith means risk. We had made an offer, but I seriously wondered if we'd gotten in over our heads. Even the credit union thought that the place was too much for us. When we'd brought the bankers out to see the place, they had told us that we should take an intermediate step first—buy a warehouse or something else that was smaller, grow some more, and *then* try for a place like the one on East Avenue.

After hearing from the financial pros, I did what I always do when I start to feel sad and down: I talked to the Lord. On July 11, I wrote in my journal, "I sensed the Lord say to me, 'Wait patiently on Me, and I will do it' (Ps. 37:5, 7)."

One day, not long after I wrote those words in my journal, I was talking on the phone in my office, and my wife walked in. She sat down on the desk and started digging in a gift bag. In those days we had three people to an office. We were packed on top of each other. I thought the bag belonged to somebody else, so it had been sitting on my desk for two or three weeks.

I told my wife, "Stop looking in the bag. It's not mine!"

She said, "No, it's yours. There's a card here that says 'Pastor Dan.' See?" She held it up.

I was still talking on the phone. "Oh. Well, what's in the bag?"

She pulled out the tissue paper and then lifted out a little handmade wooden wishing well. It was quite detailed. It even had a small chain going down into a hole—just like a real well. It also had a sign on it that said "Water of Life."

"Oh," I said. "That's nice. Okay."

As my wife sat there, waiting for me to get off the phone, she reeled up the string in the center of the well. At the end of the string was a little piece of old, yellowed paper. On the paper was a Bible verse that somebody had taped onto it probably fifty years ago. What Bible verse? Psalm 37:7: "Rest in the LORD and wait patiently for Him."

The card in the bag had been signed by a lady named Sue Moore. Sue attended our church, so I gave her a phone call. She told me that she had been shopping in Orange County at an antique store and had seen this little wishing well way on the top floor, all the way in the back corner. She walked by it and thought, *Oh, that's cute*, and the Lord said to her, "Buy that for Pastor Dan."

Sue took the wishing well to the checkout counter along with some other things. But when the cashier started ringing up the sale, Sue changed her mind. "No, I don't want that wishing well," she told the cashier. "You can put it away." *Buying it for Pastor Dan was a silly idea*, she thought.

Sue walked out the door, and the Lord said to her, as big as day, "I told you to buy that. Go back in and buy it right now."

She thought, *Whoa!* So she went back in and bought that wishing well. She took it home and put it in a gift bag with a bunch of tissue paper and then set it on my desk. That wishing well sits next to Pastor Rolo's cocoa can in my office today.

That is called confirmation. Whenever we trust God and take risks, He drops little bread crumbs in front of us, whispering in our ear, "Keep following." I didn't know where we were going as a church, but God did. And He wasn't going to tell me. He wanted me to believe that He was in our midst, listening to us, and that He was going to break forth in the miraculous.

FAITH IS SPELLED W-A-I-T

1997

On July 26, 1997, I wrote in my journal, "Received word Friday 1:45 p.m., 4:45 p.m. Washington D.C. time: we have a deal at $3.1 million as well as Evangelical Christian Credit Union loan approval at $2.8 million with stipulations. We're excited."

We thought we'd gotten a great deal on the property. We had negotiated all the fine points and agreed to terms with the owners of Rancho Lindo Community Psychiatric Centers (CPC). At the end of the day, however, we had one final detail to decide: who was going to mow the lawn while the property was in escrow?

I was sitting at my desk one day when Peter Felsch handed me the paperwork for the deal with this final matter pending. "It's CPC's property," I said. "They have to pay to mow the lawn, not us."

Peter said, "Yeah, but you don't want this to ruin the whole thing."

"No, this is an issue of principle," I insisted. "Send it back to them and tell them to mow the lawn!" So he did.

I knew the moment that I decided to hold my ground that the agreement might not come back. But I also knew this: if God was in that plan, it *would* come back.

Now faith grows people, and faith grows life, and faith grows possibility, but we don't get faith without waiting. In fact, I have found that faith is often spelled W-A-I-T. Anything good is going to take time—and it will stretch us.

Why does God make us wait? Because He's trying to build faith in us. Remember what the Bible says in Hebrews 11:6: "Without faith it is impossible to please Him, for he who comes to God must believe that He is and that He is a rewarder of those who seek him."

This thing that we call faith is both future and unseen. Hebrews 11:1 says, "Faith is the assurance of things hoped for." That means that the reward of faith is in the future. We can't see it, and God makes us wait for it. Waiting is often a test that teaches us about our hearts. If our hearts are in Jesus, we will wait for Him. If not, we will run to other places for immediate help. Waiting declares, "There is nowhere else to go but You, God!" This builds faith.

So just like that, we sent back the deal, and we waited. We were negotiating with a corporation, so we knew that it would take time. We waited weeks.

In August 1997, a month after we had sent the deal back, we heard that a company called Vencor, a huge conglomerate that was taking over hospitals all over America, had done a corporate merger and taken over CPC. That made us pretty nervous. We kept waiting.

In the meantime we had started a campaign called Inherit the Land to raise money to buy the East Avenue property. I preached to the church for weeks about sacrificing financially to see God do something miraculous in us. We planned to have a commitment Sunday on October 19, when people would sign a pledge for the amount that they felt the Lord wanted them to give.

I wrote in my journal on September 3,

> A lot has happened since last entry five weeks ago. Most of it is negative. Vencor bought out CPC, and we still don't have a purchase agreement. Worst of all, though my faith has held up to here, I am very distressed by the Inherit the

> Land campaign and having doubts as to whether or not to even proceed with the process. Leaders' meeting is Sunday, September 7, to kick off, and we may be out of the East Avenue property picture at that time. My heart has grown weary of the lack of direction I feel from the Lord. Am I to press on or wait? Please, Father, speak. Don't allow me to deceive myself and hurt or manipulate Your people. Direct my steps as only You can.

The answer to my question, of course, was that we should press in *and* wait! That's always the answer. We push into God, and we keep pushing into God, and we wait on Him to work. God had given us a prophetic word that He would give us an inheritance for the land, and then we had ended up with Helen Lovett's estate. But that had been the easy part. The hard part was getting in escrow so that we could actually buy the land.

On September 24, I went to The Church On The Way in Van Nuys to take a class taught by Pastor Jack Hayford. Over the years he and I had developed a close relationship, and he had taken me under his wing and mentored me. I had lunch with him that day, which turned out to be a sovereign, divine appointment. As we ate together, I was called away to a phone call.

It was Peter Felsch. "What's up, Peter?" I asked.

"Dan, I need to tell you that Vencor just took the property from us."

"You're kidding me."

"I'm not kidding. They called us and said that the deal's off, the escrow's over, we don't get the property. They're going to use it for a recovery hospital."

I went back to the table and sat down as forlorn as I've ever been in my life. Commitment Sunday was only three and a half weeks away, on October 19. But now I had to go to church on the last Sunday of September and break the news that we didn't have a building to buy.

Telling the church that the sale had fallen through wasn't the hardest part. I had an even bigger problem: I had to decide if God was God or if He wasn't. If I really believed Him, we would still have the commitment Sunday. "Lord," I prayed, "what are we supposed to do?"

I told Pastor Jack what had happened. As usual, he had a challenging but helpful word for me: "Go home and tell them to give, because God will do it. In fact, you watch and pray for that building, because He'll give it back to you for less money than you were going to buy it this time."

Pastor Jack went on to tell me a story about the west campus of Church On The Way, which we were sitting in that day. "We bought this building, then we lost it, but we got it back two years later for a million dollars less," he said. "Believe God for it, Dan. Don't quit believing, and believe that you will get it for less."

I thought, *Oh, that is super cool. How am I supposed to go back and tell my church that?* That's really what I thought. I didn't know if we were ever going to see the East Avenue land. Actually, I felt like I didn't know anything.

On October 1, 1997, I wrote, "On Wednesday, September 24, Vencor called and withdrew the East Avenue property from sale. The pits! We went from the top of the mountain to the valley in two days, but hopefully we will land at the foot of the cross, for that is where God wants us to be."

When you start to believe God for unseen things, generally things seem to go from bad to worse. And that's what happened.

A few days later Peter broke the news to me that he was moving back to Australia in two weeks. I had thought that God had brought Peter here to build a building. He was an engineer with a master's degree in administration.

The day after Peter delivered this unanticipated news, I wrote, "Lord, we have no land, no offering in, no building plan, and now Pete's leaving. I don't understand what You're doing. On one hand, I feel led to press forward, but as I do, everything disappears. Possibilities seem small. Help me to trust You."

In his book *Disappointment with God*, Philip Yancey writes, "Faith means believing in advance what will only make sense in reverse." I related to the idea. Nothing was making sense at that moment! But I somehow believed that God would help us, even though I had no idea what He had in mind. So on October 19, our commitment Sunday, I went to church and told everybody, "We don't have a building to make an offer on, but I would still like you to commit." You know what those people did? They stepped up and committed $665,000 to buy a piece of property that they couldn't see. That was a miracle. That is called faith.

As we make decisions to follow the dream that God places in our hearts, we can expect delay.

Let me tell you something about me. I am not special to God. I mean, I'm not more special than anybody else. Everybody is special to God. You are special to God. God wants to bless *you* and use *you*. It was the faithful sacrifice, prayer, and giving of the people at Water of Life that God used to build our church.

It would be another year before we even talked about the East Avenue land again. But that is how God often works. As we make decisions to follow the dream that God places in our hearts, we can expect delay. Noah waited 120 years from the time he started building the ark until it began to rain. Abraham was told that he would be the father of a great nation, and he didn't have Isaac until he was ninety-nine. God told Moses that he would lead his people out of four hundred years of slavery, but then He made him wait in the desert forty years.

In Habakkuk God says, "These things I plan won't happen right away. Slowly, steadily, surely, the time approaches when the vision will be fulfilled" (Hab. 2:3, TLB). We hate to wait! But remember this: a delay is not a denial. God's delay never destroys His purpose.

GOD OF THE ELEVENTH HOUR

1998–1999

I kept praying, "Where are we going to go, God?" For more than a year our attendance had been at over a thousand, and we were totally out of room. Everybody was tired of setting up and taking down chairs; our church had quit growing; we didn't have enough room for the kids. The staff was all over me. "Pastor Dan, we've got to do something!"

In the fall of 1998, Vencor, facing some challenges of its own, put the East Avenue property back on the market. This time it was listed at $3.5 million. We had serious discussions about trying to buy it, but we had been in escrow the first time at $3.1 million, and even that had been beyond our means. We decided against making an offer at the higher price. Vencor sold the property to a recovery hospital that September.

I fell into a depression from September to January that was probably as deep as I've ever been in. I couldn't believe that God would set us up and then wipe us out. We had started praying for a property in 1995—three years earlier. I was upside down in my heart with God, just crawling on the ground.

Psalm 27:13 is one of my favorite verses: "I would have despaired unless I had believed that I would see the goodness of the LORD in the land of the living." Sometimes we need to be reminded that we will see God's goodness here on Earth, in the land of the living, and not just in heaven.

But here's the thing: timing is critical. It's the key to everything in the kingdom of God. The Lord will not pick the fruit until it's ripe. He won't do something until it's time to do it. It doesn't matter if you think it's time or I think it's time or everybody else thinks it's time. If God doesn't think it's time, it's not happening yet.

The sooner we surrender to God's timing, the happier Christians we're going to be. Circumstances may make it look as if our dreams are over, but God doesn't abandon us. He's still at work. The Bible is full of promises that seemed to take too long to fulfill: Abraham and Sarah and Isaac. Zacharias and Elizabeth and John the Baptist. God says, "You watch, and I'll do it."

A. W. Tozer writes, "At the root of the Christian life lies a belief in the invisible. The object of the Christian's faith is unseen reality." See, faith is the bridge between our unseen reality and God—between our restlessness and God's peace, between our anxiety and God's presence exploding in our midst. Faith is the key, and without it, it's impossible to please God.

During this season in my life, I went to an Asian prayer summit in Los Angeles. Yes, at six foot eight I was the tallest guy in the room. A friend of mine, a man named Him Djuhana, was also there. He introduced me to Kay Hiramine, a man who at that time was the executive director for the Wagner Leadership Institute and C. Peter Wagner's assistant. Kay told me that he was on his way to a workshop to pray, so he and I spoke only briefly.

But as I turned to walk away, Kay grabbed me by the arm. "Are you looking for a building?" he asked.

I said, "Don't even go there. I don't want to talk about buildings."

But Kay didn't quit. "Pastor, I've got to tell you something. When I turned around to walk away after meeting you, God gave me this picture of a big white building with a huge library. Do you have a huge library at your church?"

Obviously Kay had no way of knowing that the School of Theology had a massive library that we had planned for them to house in a wing of the single-story building at East Avenue. When Kay said that to me, God told me, "Dan, don't give up. Don't give up! Keep believing, even though you don't see it. I will do it in My time."

Encouraged by the encounter with Kay, I redoubled my efforts. I started making phone calls. Before long Doug Curnutte at Vencor in Louisville and I had a weekly joke going. I'd call Doug, and he would laugh. That was the joke. I'd say, "Hey Doug, this is Pastor Dan at Water of Life," and he would laugh at the other end of the phone. "What do you want, Dan? The building's sold."

I'd say, "Doug, I really think God wants us to have it."

He'd say, "Dan, if you were going to buy the building, what would you pay for it?"

"I could pay you $2.5 million. That's what we could afford to do right now."

He would start laughing. "I've already got it sold for $3.5 million. Why would I sell it to you for $2.5 million?" Then he would say, "Call somebody else."

So I did. I called Kmart! I said to God, "I'm so stupid—we're never going to get East Avenue. I'm going to leave Doug alone. I'm going to go over and buy the empty Kmart building at Foothill and Haven." It was a blue light special, let me tell you. So we put $50,000 down on the Kmart property.

We brought an architect in and started making plans, and we began taking the people in the church to the site and saying, "Isn't Kmart great!"

But the entire time we were doing this, we were torn. Vencor was telling us that it was essentially a 100 percent chance that we would *never* own the East Avenue property. Kmart, on the other hand, really wanted us to take their building, because no one else wanted to buy it. Kmart kept throwing in all kinds of offers to sweeten the deal. It was a huge battle for us to believe that we could get East Avenue, which offered us much more opportunity than Kmart did and was much bigger than what our vision for Water of Life had been.

But the Kmart chapter became very strategic in our church's life, because it forced the issue. The money we'd put down on the Kmart building was going to go hard on January 10, 1999, meaning that if we changed our minds after that date, we would lose the fifty grand we'd put down.

One day I was praying when God said to me, "Kmart is your Ishmael."

As I reached for the phone, my wife said, "Happy birthday. God gave you the building."

See, Abraham had had two sons: Ishmael and Isaac. Ishmael had been born of human effort, in the flesh; he was the result of Abraham's attempt to help God out with His promise that He would give Abraham a son. Isaac, on the other hand, had been born as a result of God's promise, in the power of the Spirit. When God says to you, "That's an Ishmael," it is not a happy day.

God had spoken, so I started calling Doug Curnutte at Vencor again.

I called the week before Christmas and said, "Doug, listen, we're getting into a really bad situation. The $50,000 we've put down on Kmart is going to go hard, and we're not going to be able to buy your building."

He laughed. "Dan, our building is not going to be your building. You're never going to own this building! Give it up."

"Well, listen, Doug, what about the other guy? You told me that the deal was going to close in October. It's now December, and you've never closed the deal."

"It's done, Dan, 98 percent it's done. The guy's getting his loan."

"Call him, Doug. I don't think he's going get his loan."

He said, "Okay, I'll call you back." He never called me back. In eighteen months of me calling him, he *never* called me back.

On January 4, I called, and Doug again told me, "It's a 98 percent chance that the property is sold. You're never going to see it, Dan. Let it go."

I went back to God and said, "God, we're never going to see the property. It's not going to happen."

And God said to me, "Trust Me. Believe Me. Don't give up. Yield to Me."

So I did. On January 7, I called Doug again. We were three days away from our deadline with Kmart.

"Look," Doug said. "It's sold! It closes in the next day or two." He was emphatic.

"It hasn't closed escrow," I countered. "If it had closed escrow, I wouldn't be calling you. I'm going to keep calling you until you close the deal." I was polite but determined.

The next morning, at 6:45, I was sitting in the corner of my bedroom at my desk reading my Bible. It was January 8. My birthday. My son knocked on our bedroom door, walked in with the phone in his hand, and said, "Dad, some guy from Louisville, Kentucky, named Doug is calling you."

Doug *never* called me.

As I reached for the phone, my wife, who was lying in bed listening to this conversation, sat up and said, "Happy birthday. God gave you the building."

I picked up the phone, and Doug Curnutte said, "The guy just lost his financing. You really want the building?"

"Yeah, I really want the building."

"Okay, how much will you give me?"

I thought, *Oh no, Jack Hayford said we would get it for less. We were in escrow at $3.1 million, so it has to be less. But Lord, if I offer less, he might say no!* But I said, "Doug, I already told you—$2.5 million."

Doug yelled back over the phone, "Two and a half million? You're crazy. That property is worth $5 million right now."

"Yeah, but we're offering real money, and we can close in sixty days."

"Okay, sold," Doug said. "Write me an offer in the next three hours."

On January 30, 1999, against all odds, we opened escrow for the second time on the East Avenue property. ISOT joined us again, and we were back on track. *Thank You, God!*

But the hardest part was yet to come. That escrow lasted for three months, and it was horrific. For starters, when other groups that had tried to buy the East Avenue property heard that Water of Life had gotten a deal, they wanted in on the action. One was a much larger church than ours, and they wanted to buy us out of escrow. It was a temptation, but we held onto the escrow and to what we thought God was doing with us.

Then one morning, about two and a half months into the escrow, our Inherit the Land team was in a prayer meeting when one lady said, "Pastor Dan, I was on the Internet yesterday, and I saw Vencor's stock drop from $10.50 a share seven months ago to $.51 yesterday. They're talking about going bankrupt." That didn't sound like good news.

I asked, "If they go bankrupt, what happens?

Someone told me, "They freeze all their assets, and the bankruptcy court takes everything off the market."

What do you think I felt like? A yoyo or what?

I called up our banker as fast as I could. "Listen, I know that this is a six-month deal, and we're four months into it, but can you close in five days?"

He said, "Are you kidding?"

I said, "I'm serious."

We owe a huge thank-you to the Evangelical Christian Credit Union. They worked every night that week, and when I walked into their office, they had twelve people, four of them lawyers, at the table with paperwork at least eighteen inches deep. That's no exaggeration.

We called Vencor to see if we could close early. It was a Wednesday, and the phone rang—and rang—and rang. No answer. No answer on a Wednesday morning at a billion-dollar corporation's headquarters. This was a bad sign. I panicked. I flipped. "God, no, Lord, don't let them go into bankruptcy. Just give us five days to close this deal!"

I asked one of our staff members to call Doug Curnutte at home. "Doug!" our staff member said anxiously. "We want to close in five days!"

Does God wait until the eleventh hour, the fifty-ninth minute? Yes. He does.

Doug said, "That's no problem."

Our representative said, "Really? You mean you guys aren't going bankrupt?"

"No," Doug said. "What would make you think that we're going bankrupt?"

"Well," he said, "nobody answered the phone!"

Doug started laughing again—he always laughed at us—and said, "It's Kentucky Derby week! This is Louisville. Everybody closes during Kentucky Derby week in Louisville! You guys are nuts!"

On May 1, 1999, we closed escrow on East Avenue.

It is so important to see God's hand right at the last minute. Were we scared? We were scared. Is God good? All the time. Does He wait until the eleventh hour, the fifty-ninth minute? Yes. He does. That does not mean that He is not for us. It doesn't mean that He doesn't love us. It's in our distress that He enlarges us.

Within two or three weeks of closing escrow on East Avenue, contractors broke ground to build houses just north of our new property. They wanted to buy us out for $150,000. But after all we'd been through, we had no intention of letting the land go.

This wasn't just about a building or a piece of land. Rather, the acquisition of the East Avenue property was a memorial to all of us that God keeps His word. He always has, and He always will.

LOOKING BACK: Water of Life Through the Years

The Carrolls circa 1988: Gale, Dan, Shane, and Katie

Pastor Dan's basketball buddies and their wives filled this cocoa can with donations, asking him to become their pastor.

Our first outreach team! We went to Malaysia and Borneo in 1990. The little guy at the front of the boat is now a Water of Life pastor—my son, Shane.

2/3/97

Dear Danny,

I was praying this morning about the building and was impressed with these verses Psalm 37:7-11 (especially v. 9 + 11).

Since I'm such a cheap-skate, I never ask for a low price, I always ask for free - so the word "inherit" really stuck out to me.

I will couch all of this in "Water-of-Life-ese": I don't know if this means anything to you, but maybe the LORD is speaking to you at some level :)

Call me if you think it might help.

One of your intercessors,

Holly Moore

Holly Moore wrote me this note in 1997. It was prophetic for Water of Life.

At Water of Life we pray. Here we are gathered to intercede for the purchase of the East Avenue property.

Best friends: the Felsches (Cheryl and Peter) and the Carrolls (Dan and Gale) met at YWAM in Hawaii.

B6 Religion

Daily Bulletin, Saturday, August 21, 1999

Church, its seminary on move to Fontana

By Cathy [illegible]
Special to the Daily Bulletin

A church and seminary have found a new home, side-by-side, ensconced among the new homes highlighting the changing face of the city.

"I believe there's two Fontanas, new and old. The new Fontana is quite progressive, and that's what we'll be a part of," said Donald A. Weaver, president of the International School of Theology in San Bernardino. "With the move, our current enrollment of 85 students could double in the next three or four years."

The school, which was opened in 1978 by Campus Crusade for Christ founder William R. Bright, has several affiliated locations all over the world including Singapore, Amman, and Nairobi.

At its main campus in San Bernardino, however, IST was forced to find a new home when the property it has leased for 21 years was sold.

Deciding where to move was a difficult one, Weaver said.

"A large church in Palm Desert actually offered to have us on their property rent-free," he said. "But the school board had to ask whether that was really the best place to relocate. After doing a demographic study, we found that Fontana would be the best place to go in order to reach the greatest number of people."

> "I believe there's two Fontanas, new and old. The new Fontana is quite progressive, and that's what we'll be a part of."
>
> **Donald A. Weaver, president of the International School of Theology in San Bernardino**

The school found its home on the land belonging to the Water of Life Community Church, which is nondenominational like the seminary.

"That was just one of the things that made us compatible," Weaver said. "However, we are still separate organizations, with our own respective ministries."

Water of Life began eight years ago as a Bible-study group and grew into a church. The congregation, which has been meeting in the gym of Ruth Musser Middle School, will be moving into its first permanent location on East Avenue.

Senior Pastor Danny Carroll says he is excited about the connection between the two organizations.

"To start with, I'm a graduate of IST, and Donald and I are good friends," Carroll said. "It will also be a great way to extend both of our ministries and help us network with other people."

With Water of Life's emphasis on community outreach, Carroll admits he hopes seminary students will be encouraged to work in the church's ministries.

"I think it will be a great advantage for our students to serve in this church," Weaver said. "We want them to have a practical application to their studies, so they'll be prepared to serve when they graduate."

He believes IST, which is scheduled to open later this month, will be a valuable addition to Fontana.

"Our library, which contains 50,000 volumes, will be open to all members of the public," Weaver said. "And as the only accredited seminary in Fontana, I think we'll be able to serve more students than ever before."

Justine Frazier/Staff Photographer

ON THE MOVE: Donald A. Weaver stands in front of the new International School of Theology, which is relocating to Fontana.

A local newspaper tells the story of Water of Life and ISOT moving to East Avenue.

Our first big building project at East Avenue was our original worship center.

Dan Carroll receives the key to the city of Fontana from then-mayor Mark Nuaimi.

One of the first steps for new believers at Water of Life is to be baptized.

Pastor Jack Hayford and his wife Anna join us for the dedication of our original worship center in 2000.

The two-story building on our campus once housed the International School of Theology.

Our Times (Ontario)

Rancho church team braves hard times to help hurricane victims

Teens, adults say physical discomfort is small price for helping Honduran villagers.

DARLA MARTIN TUCKER
Our Times

HANDOUT PHOTO

Members of the Water for Life Church in Rancho Cucamonga stand next to a house they built in Honduras for a family whose home was destroyed by floods that came with Hurricane Mitch.

RANCHO CUCAMONGA — They would all go back in a heartbeat, they said, if they had the means to do it. They would gladly brave the mosquito and sand flea bites, jellyfish stings, sprained ankles, cuts, heat, humidity, random gunshots, no plumbing, and no privacy again for the sake of the villagers whose gratitude, they said, made it all worth it.

Last month, for 13 days, a group of 10 high school students and four adults from the Water of Life Church in Rancho Cucamonga lived and worked in the Honduran village of Monjaras. Six and a half days a week they worked from 7:30 a.m. to around 5 p.m. helping to build homes for villagers whose adobe and wood structures had been wiped out by floods from last fall's Hurricane Mitch.

"If I could find the funds, I would go back tomorrow," said Gary Carson, a merchandiser for Smart & Final who went on the mission trip with his son, Daniel, 16. ""It meant that much to me."

in village community center, 55 people in all, where cleanup was done in groups by gender in an open bathing area, where eight fans barely cut the heat, and where privacy was nonexistent. But they still contend it was worth it. Carson said he encountered a

bound together by black plastic. The group visited with the family, ate with them, and prayed a blessing on the house. They gave the children a pinata, and a bucket of toiletry items such as toothbrushes and soap. And they gave the family a wooden dining table

A local newspaper wrote an article about Water of Life's team that went to New Orleans to help after Hurricane Katrina struck that city.

This short-term outreach team served at a clinic in Aba, Nigeria, with Pastor Friday Nnah.

This Water of Life short-term outreach team lived the call by serving at the Joy Springs School in the Kibera slum of Nairobi, Kenya.

In January 2014, Fontana mayor Acquanetta Warren joined Gale and Pastor Dan for the groundbreaking of our new worship center.

For Easter 2014, all services and venues met together in a huge tent erected in our parking lot.

For Easter 2015, we all came together for services in the new but unfinished worship center for a pre-opening celebration.

Jeremy Camp (center) joined us for our twenty-fifth anniversary celebration in Glen Helen Regional Park in August 2015.

Our new home: the three-thousand-seat Water of Life worship center opened in November 2015. Now we can serve even more people!

NEW BUILDING, NEW GROWTH

1999–2003

In the summer of 1999, we began constructing a worship center on East Avenue that would seat eight hundred people. We planned to hold two services in the new worship center and children's classes in the existing single-story building, which meant that we could accommodate more than sixteen hundred people each weekend.

While we built, the seminary moved into the two-story building. They also moved their huge library into the north wing of the one-story building, which they were leasing from us.

The worship center building project ran into one challenge after another. We discovered one the biggest problems one day when it rained and water started dripping through the walls. Worse, the project took much longer to complete than we had anticipated, and the deadline for finishing was crossed several times.

If we hadn't decided to have regular and sustained prayer meetings several nights a week, I doubt that we ever would have seen God win this battle. God calls on His people to participate with Him, and during this season our people grew deeper and wider than I had ever seen them grow before. Intercessory prayer became our lifeblood. It kept us all on track with God in spite of all the frustrations that come along with any building project.

We were hit with one delay after another, and I struggled as I grew increasingly frustrated. Deciding to take matters into my own hands, I sent out a mailer to people in the community announcing that we were going to open on Easter Sunday of 2000. That created pressure on the construction crew to complete the job.

Several nights before Easter the work still wasn't done, so I called in a bunch of guys from our church. We went into the new building and worked until three in the morning, wiring fifteen overhead lights.

Our "help" didn't go over very well with the contractor—or with the Lord. God used that little incident to teach me. The day after we wired the lights, He rebuked me and told me never to jump in like that again. My job was to be a pastor, not the contractor. I was to trust other people to do their jobs.

Bible colleges and seminaries don't offer classes in how to construct a new sanctuary. Perhaps that is why so many of us in the ministry struggle with building projects. God's lesson for me during this time was about surrendering to His will and submitting to His desires, not my own.

(And you thought that I had learned this lesson when God told me no about moving to Malaysia! Well, surrendering our desires so that we can walk in His will is not just a lesson; it is a class that we take all our life. God is patient to teach us, even when we are not eager to learn.)

Our first service in the new worship center was on Good Friday, April 21, 2000. The place was packed. We had only a cement floor, no screens up front, nothing fancy, but the people just went nuts. They were so excited.

The move to East Avenue was the start of a new season for us. We looked for ways to reach out to the community, and we grew like crazy.

In September 2000, we celebrated our ten-year anniversary as a church. Jack and Anna Hayford joined us, and Pastor Jack brought us an encouraging word:

> One of the nice things, having the privilege of invitations like this, is that you get to come and enjoy a great work that God is doing, and you just get to be part of the fun. I feel like Anna and I are invited royalty—we get to just come in and enjoy the fun, and you folks have gone through an enormous building program, a great sacrifice and dedication and work adjusting, developing not only this facility but adjusting the existing facilities to serve your purposes. We've heard the report of the miracle of how God gave you this property, and as Dan told me, it parallels so closely a thing that the Lord did for us. It's very heart touching not only to see something that is so thriving and vibrant but to have parallel stories with you of testimonies of God's goodness. Thank you for the invitation to be here on this special day, and congratulations to all of you for your pursuit of the will and way of the Lord and the faith that's been essential to bring you to this point.

We began to fill our new space and expand our borders. One of our first outreaches was starting a preschool. YWAM operated preschools all over world, so I thought, *That would be a great way to get people from the community into our church.* In September 2000, we started with four kids! At the start of the second year, we had ninety-one. In the third year we expanded to include elementary grades. With 151 students enrolled, Water of Life Christian School was off and running.

I've long had the mindset that we should reach out to the community in creative and dynamic ways. We should not simply wait for people to come to us—we should go to them. In 2001 we did exactly that, teaming up with Los Angeles-based ministry Win Our

World International to hold our first WOW JAM. A WOW JAM is a huge all-day barbecue with music and games.

We went to a needy area of the city and offered people haircuts, groceries, bike repairs, and other services. It was like one big party with people worshiping in the street and even being baptized. Before long we were doing WOW JAMS all over the area—we even did several in Detroit and New York.

The WOW JAMS made Water of Life visible in the community, not only giving us a chance to reach out but also bringing many new people into our services. As we grew, we needed a way to help everyone grow spiritually and to connect with one another.

Saddleback Church pastor Rick Warren provided a perfect tool to help. In 2002 he released *The Purpose Driven Life*, and we used the book to help launch a giant small-group outreach. We trained leaders, recruited hosts, and saw groups of ten to twenty people or so start meeting in homes around the Inland Empire. With that initiative we added fifty to seventy groups to our church that never went away.

In the fall of that year Jeff Keller, who went on to direct our kids' ministry, came to me with an idea called Trunk or Treat. He had seen it done at his former church and asked if he could do one at Water of Life. Jeff tried to explain how people would decorate their car trunks on Halloween night and park them in the church lot. Children from all over would come to have fun and collect candy in a safe environment. I wasn't really tracking with the idea, but Jeff wanted to do it. "Fine, go ahead. Whatever," I told him, and he went after it.

The funny thing is, I had been praying for God to show us some kind of community outreach that our church could become known for. But I didn't connect the dots until after the event, which I hadn't attended, when Jeff told me that about three hundred people had come to our Trunk or Treat. I was really surprised. *Maybe there's something to this Trunk or Treat thing*, I thought. I told Jeff, "Next year let's do this as a church." Within two years, we had six thousand people attending. (At our 2015 event more than ten thousand people showed up!)

Water of Life was growing by leaps and bounds, but as always happens when God leads His people on a journey of faith, we had our share of uncomfortable moments.

I was really surprised.
***Maybe there's something to this Trunk or Treat thing,* I thought.**

A year or so after we moved onto the property on East Avenue, our friends at the seminary, who had made it possible for us to buy the land and build our worship center, were seeing their dream change. Due to several unforeseen circumstances—including their founder's illness and impending death—the seminary leaders had decided to close their California campus and consolidate the school at the Campus Crusade headquarters in Florida after all, and they asked us to purchase the two-story building from them. We weren't prepared for this financially, yet as we prayed about it, God confirmed that this was part of His plan. So we flexed, and we believed God for the $1.2 million needed for the transaction.

Since Dr. Bill Bright, the founder and president of Campus Crusade, was now terminally ill, he came to Los Angeles with his wife, Vonette, to settle his affairs. While he was in the area, he called me and asked if we could meet. Dr. Bright had signed my diploma when I had graduated from ISOT, and he and I had built a relationship in the two or three years that the seminary had partnered with Water of Life, so we knew each other.

As we visited that day, he took off his watch and gave it to me as a gift. It was a millennial watch; I still have it. "Dan," he said, "I'm here because I'm dying, and we owe you hundreds of thousands of dollars on a long-term lease." He was referring to the north wing of the single story, which housed ISOT's fifty-five-thousand-volume library. "Would you release us from the lease?" he asked me.

I told him that we would. Then he said, "Dan, I want to give you the library." Wow. That was a huge thing. This was a fully accredited seminary library, worth half a million dollars, and he gave it to me in lieu of the lease payments.

So the seminary relocated to Florida, and we bought the two-story building, which brought our brief but blessed partnership with ISOT to a close. Acquiring the building actually worked out well, because we desperately needed more space. God amazingly worked out details for both ISOT and us.

Dr. Bright's gift actually led to a personal connection for me with King's Seminary. During our early years on East Avenue I worked on my doctorate at King's, which Pastor Jack Hayford had founded in 1997. One Sunday while I was still studying with King's, Pastor Jack came to preach at Water of Life. While he was with us, I felt compelled to show him our "church library." He politely declined. I understood why. Who wants to see another church library? But I insisted that he see it, playing the straight man and not giving away the surprise. As always, Pastor Jack graciously agreed, and we walked together across our campus.

When the doors swung open and he saw the entire north wing of our single-story facility packed wall to wall with a fully accredited theology library, he was certainly taken aback.

Pastor Jack asked, "Where did you get this library?"

I told him how Dr. Bright had given it to us. But there is more to the story: I hadn't shown the library to Pastor Jack to impress him. I had brought him to the north wing of our single story because the Lord had told me to give King's College and Seminary the entire library. Not only was such a vast library essential for the college and seminary to become accredited, but it also would help train future generations of pastors. That excited me most! And I got to be part of what they were doing, because not long after we donated the library to King's, I was asked to join their board of directors.

Water of Life had always been about giving, and the Lord had blessed us over and over again as we had given to His work. Now God was about to call us to give again.

One thing we had not been able to do up to this point in our story of faith was finish the floor in the worship center. After three years in our new home, we were still meeting on a cement floor! The cost to install a proper gym floor was upwards of $40,000, and we had saved about $35,000 toward making that happen. But one day as I was praying, the Lord told me that I was supposed to give the $35,000 that we had saved to another church for their building program.

"Really, Lord?" I prayed. "We've been saving for a long time for our floor."

As usual, my excuse didn't go very far. The Lord was really clear with me, so I gave the money away. Of course, then I had to tell everyone at Water of Life what I'd done.

I made the announcement at a Wednesday night service. It went something like this: "I need you to pray for provision for a floor for the worship center, because I gave away the building fund to another church." I went on to explain how the Lord had impressed upon me to give the funds away.

After the service a man named Paul Newman (not the actor!) approached me. Paul was a veterinarian who had owned several clinics in the area, and he asked, "How much will it cost to install the floor?"

"About $41,000," I responded.

"No, how much exactly," he insisted.

I told him the exact dollar figure, and Paul pulled out his checkbook and wrote a check on the spot. He and his wife, Stormie, had recently sold all their clinics, and they had been trying to decide how to tithe the money from the sales. And that's how we got our gym floor.

This was Water of Life's story of faith. We gave away our heart and time and resources to love on our community. We gave away our library instead of selling it. We gave away the money that we had saved for our worship-center floor because someone else needed it. We gave because God told us too, and then we watched Him move in miraculous ways to touch people's lives and to provide exactly what we needed.

TOUCHING NEIGHBORHOODS AND NATIONS

2003–2009

Water of Life has always been about people, not just buildings and numbers. But our growth has shown something about how God has been at work in our midst. By fall 2003 our weekend attendance had multiplied to twenty-four hundred.

To accommodate the people who were coming, we decided to create additional worship spaces for overflow on weekends. We experimented with our first venue in 2003. We called it the video café and held it in a room in the single-story building. We offered an acoustic-style worship service with a laid-back atmosphere, and we live-streamed the sermon from the main sanctuary. The venue was packed to capacity immediately.

As we continued to grow, we knew that we needed more venues and also that we needed to expand to other types of services, but that meant more buildings. In 2004 we started a campaign that we called Fulfilling Our Destiny. The campaign was designed to raise funds to build the north and south venues and the chapel, all of which were built adjacent to the original worship center.

Agua de Vida, our Spanish-language service, came next. Its first meeting was on Sunday April 4, 2004, when a group of twenty adults gathered to worship God. The service was entirely in Spanish in what was then our gym (later our west venue). Agua de Vida provided a way for us to reach Spanish-speaking people in an atmosphere in which they could feel relaxed and find relevant Bible teaching.

So much was happening on East Avenue, but we always sought to be part of the larger body of Christ and what God was doing in our community.

In 2004 Water of Life participated with more than a thousand local churches in the Greater Los Angeles Billy Graham Crusade at the Rose Bowl in Pasadena. Jack Hayford was one of the leading pastors for the Billy Graham Crusade, and I was invited to be part of the executive planning committee. Water of Life was asked to be responsible for the recruiting and training of volunteer counselors.

The thing is, I was getting ready to leave on a trip to Cambodia and Thailand, so I asked my assistant, Susan DePaola, to go to the planning meetings for me. We had just hired Susan, so I kind of threw her into the deep end and sent her off to meet with people such as Lloyd Ogilvie, a former Senate chaplain, and Martha Williamson, executive producer of the *Touched by an Angel* television show. Susan had no idea what she was getting into when she started working for me!

The planning and preparation for the Crusade took months, which meant that there were lots of meetings. Susan represented Water of Life so well that the Graham team asked me if she could help not only with the sixty-five hundred volunteer counselors but also with the entire event. Susan worked hand in hand with the Billy Graham team, and the Crusade was amazing.

Susan has been with Water of Life for twelve years now. Wow. Time goes by fast! Needless to say, she has done more to touch and change lives than any of us around here ever imagined possible. And Susan isn't the only one—over the years the Lord has sent us many people, like Linda Jones, Bob Bryant, and Vicky Anderson, among others, who have jumped into various kinds of service and have blessed us tremendously. The truth is, none of us ever really knows what God is up to until we jump into the deep end and begin to swim.

After the crusade God showed us more ways to reach neighborhoods and nations. When Hurricane Katrina hit New Orleans in 2005, we were ready to serve. Peter Felsch, who had returned to California by then, oversaw ministry teams that we sent to New Orleans. It was a massive effort that built and solidified our outreach in a time of national crisis and disaster.

About this time I had a little crisis of my own. Off and on for nearly five years I had been battling atrial fibrillation (called AFib in the medical profession). In layman's terms this simply means that my heart's electrical impulses were shorting out. By 2005 my heartbeat was way too fast—not just now and then but all the time. I was very sick and not sure I would be able to continue in the ministry.

That year alone Gale and I visited numerous cardiologists and four electrophysiologists. These doctors work just on the electrical impulses in the heart. Mine had jumped the track, racing between 150 and 300 beats a minute.

The Lord allows us to experience painful tests, but it isn't easy when those tests can have life-or-death consequences. For me it was especially tough because the church was growing and because I had two young children still at home.

After months of prayer for healing, waiting on the Lord, and seeking counsel from doctors and friends, I opted to fly to Ohio so that Dr. Randall Wolf of the University of Cincinnati Medical Center could perform open-heart surgery on me. Dr. Wolf is so renowned now for what he does that there is actually a Wikipedia page about his work, but at that time he had done only about 250 surgeries for AFib. It was clear to me that this was a very dangerous procedure. In fact, so dangerous that I planned my funeral service before the surgery in case I didn't make it through.

This was one of those moments that caused me to take account of my life. It was also a time when I realized how many people really cared about Gale and me. Water of Life was more than our home—it was our family.

During the eight hours of open-heart surgery and over the weeks that followed, thousands of people prayed for us and for my healing. Amazingly, three weeks after the surgery, my heart converted to a normal rhythm and has never had an irregular pace since. This episode was certainly a test, but it ultimately became a testimony that I now give from a grateful heart.

As you can see, 2005 was a busy time. That was also the year we hosted our first men's barbecue. It was rather simple. About twenty-five guys came to my house. We put the tailgates of our trucks down, set barbecues out on the driveway, and had Bible study and a cookout.

The next spring we did the same thing. The men started inviting other guys, and the annual event went from twenty-five to fifty to a hundred to two or three or four hundred. Finally we started ordering catered food and being intentional about it. We've held the barbecue at my house every year since, and in 2015 we expanded to two nights. More than fourteen hundred men showed up. (Yes, I have a big yard!)

By Easter 2005, when sixty-four hundred people attended Water of Life throughout the weekend, we were literally bursting at the seams. In 2006 we opened our three new onsite venues, which enabled us to move our video café into the south venue and to start two new services: one in the chapel with traditional hymns and the other in the north venue with rock-and-roll music (this eventually became Soul Celebration, our gospel music service). The next year we added the south parking lot. All this expansion helped, but we were again operating at near capacity.

Despite all this vibrant ministry, the recession of 2008 and the toll it took on the banking industry hit us hard. The year following the economic downturn was a tough one—economically, spiritually, and emotionally. None of us had ever been through anything like it before, and it impacted Water of Life in every way. But discouragement can be blinding and deafening—it can destroy the work of God and faith. Dismay can come out of exhaustion, physically, emotionally, spiritually, but the outcome is always the same: distance from God. We needed to beware!

God was calling us, once again, to take a risk and believe beyond the circumstances that we could see.

In the midst of this recession, some of our church members lost their homes at an alarming rate. Many ended up homeless, and some of our regulars actually lived out of their cars. It was a difficult and bleak time for a lot of people.

As I always do when I don't know what to do, I prayed. As I spoke to God about people's needs, I realized that He was calling Water of Life to once again take a risk and believe beyond the circumstances that we could see. We needed to step out in faith. "But how, God?" I prayed. "How?"

We were not alone. Members of churches across the nation were hit hard, including many at Gateway Church in Texas, one of the largest churches in America, where my friend Robert Morris pastors. Pastor Robert is a trusted friend of mine, and I decided to call him and ask how his church was caring for the newly homeless and hurting people.

"We throw a party," he said.

What? A party?

Gateway had held a special event, he explained to me, and called it "God's Party." At the service they had given away thousands of dollars to help families that were in need.

What a great idea! Wow.

Our leaders at Water of Life quickly rallied around the vision, and we planned for ourselves a God Party that was second to none. A few weeks later, during Sunday morning services, I announced the plans: that evening we would have a service to minister to those among us who were hurting and impacted by the recession. No mention of money was made whatsoever.

That evening the worship center was packed. I opened the service with a short teaching on giving and receiving, then I asked anyone with overdue utility bills or other smaller payments to stand. A few people rose to their feet. I am sure that it was hard for them to admit their need. But it was an important step.

I asked everyone who was still seated to pray about paying the bills of those standing. I knew that this might be very embarrassing for some, but what took place next was beyond belief. People throughout the worship center moved about, began praying over each other, and then started writing checks. Yes, they were paying the overdue bills of those who had stood in faith.

Helping pay small bills was one thing, but what about the large payments for home mortgages, cars, and medical care? I asked people burdened by this type of bill to stand. And as I had with the small bills, I asked those still seated to pray about helping make a dent in these individuals' debts.

Again, there was movement all over the worship center as people prayed for each other and wrote more checks. Water of Life showed once again that we are givers—a miracle that I thank God for every time I see it happen.

Before we closed our God Party, I asked everyone who was standing—those who still had outstanding bills—to come to the front of the Worship Center, stand in one of five lines that we had set up, and allow us to minister to them.

Church leaders stood at the front of each line with a basket behind them, each basket containing $10,000 cash. As people reached the front of the line, we prayed over each person and his or her need, then gave each one an envelope with cash in it as we felt led by the Holy Spirit. We gave away a total of $50,000 that night. Another $50,000 changed hands between church members as individuals wrote checks, sacrificed, and served each other. More than $100,000 in immediate needs were met that evening!

This was a game changer for us. The generous giving and humble receiving broke a poverty mentality that was gripping our region. Our acts of faith—both giving and receiving—allowed us to press ahead with ministry.

So we kept building and giving, and we kept asking God to show us new ways that we could reach out to people in our community and around the world. My doctoral dissertation for King's Seminary, which I had completed recently, had been on why the suburban church in America had abandoned the poor, and that study impacted me on a deep level to think that Water of Life should be doing more to minister to those in need.

To come up with ideas, I took several teams to Dallas, Texas, for a Leadership Network conference that was designed to bring churches together and help them develop innovative ideas for building God's kingdom. I actually flew the mayor and some city council members from Fontana to one of these conferences, and I told them that I wanted to do some kind of outreach that would impact our city. We brainstormed with several other churches from around America on how to build outreach ministry, and as we listened to what others were doing, we gleaned a little here and a little there and came up with our own ideas.

In 2009 we started CityLink—a way to link our church back to the city. It was a place to feed people, train and equip them, and offer them healing and other practical helps. CityLink grew over the years to offer dozens of services and ministries to people in the Inland Empire: repairing single mothers' and widows' and elderly people's cars, distributing thousands of boxes of food each year through our food warehouse, starting a thrift store so that people in need could buy clothing and other items inexpensively, and equipping mobile medical units staffed by doctors and nurses to offer basic medical care to people who couldn't easily afford it.

CityLink ballooned to include after-school programs, ministry to pregnant teens, prison ministry, adoption and foster care, homeless ministry, Thanksgiving and Christmas food baskets, and much more.

No matter how big we got or how far we traveled, outreach at Water of Life has always been about individuals.

Outreach has always been number one for us. Even as we were launching CityLink and doing other local ministry, we were continuing to develop relationships with people and ministries around the world as well, sending out short-term teams and investing in long-term ministries.

Our international work had started with those first trips to Malaysia when we had met at La Petite. It grew over the years as we built relationships with people like Charlie and Kathy Milbrodt, who run several orphanages in Thailand that care for hundreds of children. We sent teams to the slums of Nairobi, Kenya, where Charles and Rose Wanyama run Joy Springs School. It was also natural for us to link up with Mario and Veronica Santos in Mexico and with Pastor Friday Nnah and his children's school in Nigeria. As we grew, our outreach ministry grew too.

But no matter how big we got or how far we traveled, outreach has always been about individuals. One year at Trunk or Treat, I saw a little lady named Amika Coleman walking around by herself, looking dazed and confused, which is easy to do on

Trunk or Treat night! I didn't know who she was, but I went up to her and put my arm around her and said, "Can I help you? Are you lost?"

"I'm looking for candy," she told me.

I pointed toward the correct area. "Candy's down there in the parking lot." We talked a few more moments, and I invited her to church before she went on to find what she was looking for.

A few months later I got an e-mail from Amika. She wrote, "I didn't know that you were the pastor when you put your arm around me and told me where to go that night at Trunk or Treat. But you invited me to come to church, and I came. I was not a believer, and as I sat in church, I quickly realized that I *was* what you asked me if I was that night—lost." Wow. That simple question "Are you lost?" turned out to be what God used to speak to that woman. "But I want to tell you something," her e-mail went on. "I gave my heart to Jesus Christ this year, and today I'm found."

Amika got so excited about the Lord that when she was planning to be baptized, she invited eighty people from her work, her neighborhood, her family—and forty-one of them showed up for her baptism. She had to drag three of her own kids to church, but once she got them here, she couldn't get them out of here. "Pastor Dan," she wrote, "you have no idea what has happened in my life since Trunk or Treat last year."

One life at a time, people have been touched for God's glory. And it's all because the people of Water of Life have believed beyond themselves, starting with those twenty-one in our home Bible study. These individuals have broken the mold and reached out to touch neighborhoods and nations.

When I would hook up that trailer and head off to La Petite to set up for church, I thought that I was the dumbest clown on the block. Now look at what God has done. Really! Look! It's like Kevin Bolka would say when he was setting up chairs in our early days: "If we put the chairs out, they will come." He was right! And God gets all the glory.

"CUL-DE-SACED" BY GOD

2008–2010

It was incredible to see so many people's lives being touched by God, but with all this growth we came up against the inevitable: we were out of space—again. God had so obviously given us the land on East Avenue, but now that we had four thousand people attending on weekends, we weren't sure what to do. "God," I prayed, "where are You taking us now?"

The story of Water of Life is a story of faith, but that doesn't mean that everything went smoothly. It's easy to read stories like this and get excited about the miracles, but things were a huge struggle at times, and this issue with the building just wore us out.

I took some heat when we hit tough times or faced setbacks. We had grown rapidly, yes. But our finances didn't grow as quickly. The national economy was tight, and as with most churches, this affected Water of Life's tithing and giving. We simply didn't have the finances to hire enough staff.

During this particularly difficult season, Robert Morris and I were both attending a particular conference. At one of the meetings in which he introduced me, he actually said, "This is Pastor

Danny Carroll. He has a really big church in Fontana with a really small staff."

It was that bad. In fact, it was so bad that several staff members left Water of Life, including three or four people who had been with me for eight to ten years. They remained friends, but it was still a struggle for me.

"Okay, Lord," I prayed, "I'm losing these people I really love, and I've done ministry with them a long time. But I really feel that You're in all this change and growth and that we're supposed to keep going."

I talked with our leadership about options for expanding our space at Water of Life. The obvious answer seemed to be to build a new, larger worship center on our East Avenue property, and we set out to do just that. In 2008 we embarked on the journey under the guiding title of "Until the Whole World Hears." We really had no idea of the journey that God would take us on. My journal entry about the servant leaders' Sunday night service in March 2008 records what I thought the Holy Spirit had spoken to me that night: "This will be a wild ride, unlike any you have been on." That has certainly proved to be true!

With the new campaign fourteen hundred faith-filled people pledged a total of $11 million to build a new sanctuary on the corner at East Avenue. We had plans drawn up, but when we did a traffic study to see if our property and the surrounding streets would be able to handle the increased number of vehicles and people that the new building would seat, the answer was no. Disappointingly, we had to abandon the plan. To this point we had never expected to move from East Avenue, but suddenly it seemed that we needed to.

Our building plans laid aside, we spoke to a Christian financier who bought shopping centers and turned them into churches, which led to our contacting the owners of the Foothill Village Shopping Center. That conversation ended several months later, however, when the owners wanted a sixty-day escrow and we refused to move that quickly.

In September 2009, the elder board approved construction of a building on the north end of our property, which would have been opposite the location of our first worship center, for $1.5–$2.5 million. After working on plans, the cost estimate came in at closer to $5 million, so we closed that option down, not wanting to go beyond our means.

Buying Etiwanda Gardens, a property just half a mile west of East Avenue, was another option. We nearly made an offer for it, but once again God shut that door.

We even went over to Victoria Gardens to try to rent an offsite venue there. We were initially given the green light by the shopping center management, but the decision was overruled by city officials, and that door was closed as well.

At that point we were five for five—or zero for five, depending on how you calculate it. We felt like we were driving bumper cars, constantly moving in new directions only to bump into a wall and be bounced back. We started to realize that God, in His wisdom, had "cul-de-saced" us.

"Cul-de-saced" is a little phrase I use to describe life when God leads His people into a dead-end street. That happened to the apostle Paul in Acts 16 when he was prevented from going into Asia and instead was ultimately led to Europe via a vision. It was comforting to me to know that even the apostle Paul was sometimes at a loss as to where the Spirit was directing him to go.

This happened to Moses as well when he had led the Israelites to the Red Sea and had nowhere to turn when Pharaoh and his armies came to attack them. No doubt God intentionally directed Israel into a cul-de-sac at the sea in order to display His power and possibility: "The LORD spoke to Moses, saying, 'Tell the sons of Israel to turn back and camp before Pi-Hahiroth, between Migdol and the sea.'... Pharaoh will say of the sons of Israel, 'They are wandering aimlessly in the land; the wilderness has shut them in'" (Exod. 14:1–3).

The people of Israel must have realized when Moses led them to this place that outwardly it appeared to be a disaster in the making. But Exodus 14:4 says that "they did so"—in other words, they obeyed. And God led them right into a cul-de-sac.

The pressure of Water of Life's cul-de-sacing, along with some simultaneous personal tragedies, nearly did Gale and me in. In June 2009, in the middle of our fruitless efforts to find solutions to our space problems, we reached a point of exhaustion and decided that we were going to leave the ministry.

I called Pastor Jack Hayford and told him how I was feeling. He told me, "Anna and I have a getaway house in Solvang; without it we couldn't have survived. You need a place where you and Gale can get away."

I then called Robert Morris. Pastor Robert, like me, was on the board of King's Seminary, and it was through our connection there that he and I had become close friends. I told him that Gale and I were thinking of resigning. "Debbie and I want to meet with you for a week before you decide," he said to me.

So Gale and I flew to Texas. When we got there, Pastor Robert said, "I want you to put your wallet away. Everything this week is on us." They took us out to dinner every night, and they put us up in the Hilton Hotel. One day they took us to a home that they owned in the countryside. Pastor Robert explained to me that this was a place where he and Debbie went to recoup, and he said that Gale and I needed a place like theirs. During the course of that week, Robert and Debbie convinced us not to leave Water of Life.

Gale and I had a cabin in Mount Baldy that we had bought with our inheritance from my parents. We had been using it as a rental property, but it was too close to home to be our getaway, so we sold it. After a short search, we bought a cabin in Bishop, California. That's where we go to rest.

That trip to Texas was a lifesaving one for Gale and me, and it indebted us to Robert and Debbie at a very deep level. People like Pastor Jack and the Morrises have helped us along the way, giving us the vision and insight that we have needed in times when we have felt like giving up. I often say that we all need friends for those times when we hit bumps in the road of life. Without the Morrises and the Hayfords and many others like them, there is no doubt that Gale and I would have left the ministry long ago.

The situation Water of Life was in during this season was the most trying one we had faced in the almost ten years since we had moved to East Avenue. But it's never an accident when God leads us to a dead end. It is when we are faced with very difficult circumstances that God works both in us and through us, and Gale and I learned that lesson once again right along with the people of Water of Life.

I had been sure that we were done growing, but more people kept coming. The growth had to be God!

Water of Life existed for one reason: to reach and touch and redeem people. That was why we kept growing. But in order to keep doing what we had been called to do, we needed facilities. We had never set out to get big. Remember, I had set out to obey God and then get outta California! When we had grown to 250 people, I had been overwhelmed. I remember thinking, *I want to keep this small—I like it this way*. When we had crossed a thousand, I had been sure that we were done growing, but more people kept coming. The growth had to be God! Just as His ideas had been different from mine when the church first started, so now He had different ideas for our church building than we did.

The question set before us now was, should we step back or step up—stay safe or press in? I had always been of a mind to press in. That's what we had done over a decade earlier when we had been in a similar situation. We had stepped out in faith and looked at every building we could find in Rancho Cucamonga, and through that process God had brought us to East Avenue. It had not been easy, but our path had been orchestrated by God, just as Moses' and Paul's paths had been. Our decision now wasn't really about whether to build a new building or move to another property. It was about journeying with God. Were we willing to follow—even though we didn't know where He was taking us?

Toward the end of 2009, John Vaughn, a seminary professor who wrote for *Outreach* magazine and dealt exclusively with big churches, contacted us. He said, "You guys live under the radar—nobody knows who you are or what you're doing, and you're doing some interesting things. I'd like to come out and see you." So in January 2010, he came to East Avenue. We asked him, "Tell us what our journey looks like from your view." John did some homework on our attendance, the size of our meeting rooms, how many services we had, and so on. At that point we were running about fifty-four hundred on a weekend.

As he worked, he kept saying, "Very interesting." After crunching his numbers, John told us, "Your picture is very unique. You have the smallest sanctuary of any church over five thousand in the country. You have the biggest church in America meeting on the smallest piece of property. You put more people on a smaller spot than anyone else in America." Then he said, "People don't do what you do. It's hard for people to get to church here. It's hard to park, hard to find a seat, hard to get kids to their classes. It must be really stressful."

All our staff said, "Amen!"

"Because of your situation," John went on, "you're aborting your destiny right now. God didn't call you to be jammed in. I would bet my house, because I do this for a living, that if you had a three-thousand-seat sanctuary, you would run over eight thousand people within a year. God wants to bring people to you, but whether He can or not will depend on whether or not you will make room."

We as a church had to decide if we would reach out and make room for more people. If we did, God would bless it, and it would be part of our destiny and glory. If not, we would miss out.

In 2009 we got a phone call that would have a major impact on our destiny as a church and begin to lead us out of our cul-de-sac. A local businessman said, "I hear you're thinking about moving. I don't want you to leave Fontana; you've really impacted our community. I'll sell you a forty-acre piece of land for $5 million to help you stay here."

The property was near Sierra and Summit Avenues, about six miles from our current site, easily freeway accessible from all directions, and big enough for us to create a campus that would accommodate over 4,500 people in one gathering. It was also just down the road from my house!

The man who owned the land had bought it for $17 million, and now, partly because of the bad economy and partly because he wanted to help us out, he was offering to sell it to us for $5 million.

We thought, *Well, the economy's flatter than a pancake. Do we really want to do this?*

Our elder board went to the Sierra property to check it out. I didn't get the sense that we were to buy it, but while we were there, we gathered in a prayer circle, and everybody else—which was shocking to me—said, "We need to buy this land."

I said, "Really? You think that?"

I had to go out there by myself, walk around a few times, and pray before I got my head around the idea. Starting from scratch was not what I wanted to do. *Sell me the shopping center, sell me Etiwanda Gardens*, I thought, but I wasn't really excited about pushing dirt. But anytime we get stuck in life, we have to readjust our expectations as to what God is speaking. So I listened to our brothers on our board, whom I trust, and they unanimously said, "We need to do this."

We had one more thing to do: we needed to go back to the church and ask the people if they were okay with a change of plans. They had pledged $11 million for the Until the Whole World Hears campaign, and we needed to know if they were willing for us to redirect those funds to buy the Sierra property. The response from the congregation was overwhelmingly positive, so with that final confirmation in place, we decided to go ahead and buy that land for $5 million.

In December 2010, we deposited $250,000 in escrow for the property on Sierra. We called in Brian Conner, the architect who had helped design Saddleback Church, and began to work up plans with him. Once built, Water of Life would be able to minister to over fourteen thousand people in a weekend in just three services.

We had an aggressive plan, and it broke down into three phases: (1) pay off the land, which was just over $5 million, by our due date of June 1, 2012; (2) secure loans to help construct the initial building; and (3) sell the East Avenue campus and use the proceeds to help pay down the debt that we would incur. We hoped to pay off the land through the Until the Whole World Hears campaign, which we reenergized for our new plans, and open the Sierra campus by 2013.

That was our plan. But God had His plan. And He was about to take us on the next leg of our wild ride.

MILLION-DOLLAR MIRACLE

2010–2012

Even with the rollercoaster building situation, we kept reaching out to neighborhoods and nations and watching God bless. In the first twenty years of the church's life, rarely had a year passed that God hadn't moved with enormous power and grace, and as we moved into our twenty-first year in the fall of 2010, things were no different. We began the year with a twentieth-anniversary celebration at nearby Glen Helen Regional Park. As a church, we spent a day together, highlighted by our guest Matt Redman leading us in worship. For many thousands of us in the Water of Life family, that celebration was one of the greatest times we had yet experienced together.

That year we also kicked off our first trimester of our School of Ministry—a ministry that had been in the planning stages for three years. Much to our surprise, God moved in ways far beyond what we could have imagined. Hundreds of people joined us on Tuesday nights for three hours of equipping and training. The launch of the school was the single most powerful thing God has done in our midst in years.

For Easter 2011 we returned to Glen Helen Regional Park—and worshiped in the rain. We had rented the large outdoor amphitheater so that the entire church could meet together in one place at one time, but my feelings about the day were mixed. It was awesome to see the entire church together, but the rain-soaked service also highlighted our need for more space.

I pressed hard into prayer during that season. Special seasons tended to bring our need for a larger facility to the forefront. Offering ten services or more on Easter weekend or at Christmas was tough on all of us who served and participated, and renting another facility was costly and required a huge amount of logistical work. After all the work that our staff and servant teams did to prepare for a harvest of lives at Easter 2011 only to experience the disappointing weather, everyone understood even more why we needed a larger auditorium to reach the people God continued to bring to us.

Please don't misunderstand—God worked in great ways that Easter at Glen Helen, and we rejoiced with the outpouring of His grace on those who attended and came to the altar to receive His touch. But we also recognized even more fully the difficulty of navigating ministry in a facility that we had outgrown. So as a church we continued to press into God and sacrificially give for the land on Sierra, believing that our giving would touch thousands of lives for His glory as we sought to reach neighborhoods and nations for Him.

It was with great excitement that on each Sunday in August 2011 we took people out to walk the land at Sierra and to pray over it. But even as we waited and prayed for a new campus, we were convinced that God wanted us to continue to expand our ministry. With that conviction in mind, we again began to consider new venues and even offsite campuses. God opened a door for us in 2011 through a church that was closing its doors in Upland, located on 8th and Mountain. We signed a one-year lease on this property with two years of options.

We opened our first offsite campus at the facility in Upland on September 18, 2011, with Pastor Willie Ulibarri taking the lead as campus pastor. The first Sunday morning service was attended by more than four hundred people. We were excited, actually thrilled, to have a new opportunity to reach and touch more people! A year later we opened our second offsite campus in Rancho Cucamonga with Pastor Nico Mendez leading this new venture. So many people were getting equipped in the School of Ministry (461 in the fall of 2011) that opening new venues also offered them opportunities to put their gifts and callings to work.

By January 2012, after making payments on the Sierra property for a year, we had paid a total of $1.3 million. But we had a problem: we still owed $3.7 million, and it was due on July 1, just six months away. Because of the economic crash of 2008, the Until the Whole World Hears campaign hadn't brought in as we much money as we had anticipated it would.

In the following months I prayed about this a lot and walked this through with the Lord. "Okay, God," I said, "we've been journeying for more than a year now, and we've only been able to pay $1.3 million." That was a lot of money in those days, the economy being what it was, and certainly I would have been shortsighted and unfaithful to not think that was a lot of money. So I was always saying, "Thank You, God, thank You, God, thank You, God, $1.3 million is awesome. But we owe $3.7 million more, by the way, and oh, by the way, it's due June 1."

Inwardly I pressed in with faith. But outwardly speaking things didn't look good. At one point we met with the owner of the land, who had been very gracious to us. He told us that the due date was a "soft line," which meant that we didn't have to cross it in June, even though our contract said we did. "We'll work with you into the fall," he assured us. "If you have to remortgage your property over on East Avenue to pay this, you can do that."

I was the one who signed on the dotted line for all these things, and this was not a happy day for me. I walked and prayed a lot that spring. "God," I reminded Him often, "You have all the money that we need, but right now I don't have any."

In the midst of all this pressure-filled season, one night after services were over and everyone had gone home, I walked around our campus alone and stopped behind our onsite venues. A number of other churches had looked at our East Avenue property, and we thought we were very close to selling it.

As I gazed up at the cross on the outside of our chapel, I prayed. I said to the Lord, "Father, this place has been such a huge blessing to all of us. You have done so many wild and deep things to touch and heal people here. Thank You for this place."

God's response was immediate. I distinctly felt Him say to me, "You know, I gave you this property, and you can sell it if you want to. But it will make Me sad if you do."

It was as clear as day.

That was the first time I realized that I could do something that was not actually sin but that would make God sad. What an amazing thought—the God of the universe would allow me to do something that would sadden Him. The Lord's response to my prayer wore on me heavily. I shared it with our board of elders, and it drove us to rethink whether or not we wanted to sell our East Avenue site.

We decided to take East Avenue off the market and wait to see what God would do. This altered our plans, as we now decided that we could build only one major building on Sierra initially and would have to add other buildings later, as we could afford to do so.

That Easter, 2012, we rented a huge tent and set it up in the south parking lot. This way we could hold all our Easter services under one roof on our own property. The altar that year was packed with hungry, hurting people. We had 14,200 people attend services, and 839 of them came forward to fill out cards declaring that they had received Christ or rededicated their lives to Him. I often recalled that picture of people standing at the altar, because it was for people like this that we needed a larger worship center.

When we crossed the Sierra payment deadline on June 1, we still hadn't raised the full $5 million. In fact, we'd only been able to pay $1.5 million of it. It was a painful thing, but it wasn't the end of the world, because we had been told that it was soft, right?

On June 2, I got a phone call from the property owner's company, and they said, "We need a meeting." A couple of us went to their office building in Rancho Cucamonga, and when we walked in, it was obviously not the same atmosphere we had experienced in the restaurant with the owner. His business partner said, "Where's our money?"

I took a deep breath and, looking at the majority owner, who was sitting in the room, said, "Well, he told us that it was a soft line."

They said, "Actually, it was a hard line, and you owe us the money."

I thought, *Okay, well, the world just changed, didn't it?* The truth is, they could have foreclosed on us and taken the $1.5 million that we'd put in up to that point plus the interest—another $500,000. After all, I had signed on the dotted line.

I went home and sat down with my wife, and I said, "You know, I would hate to lose my job and the confidence of the people at Water of Life because this happened, but if it does go down that way, it goes down that way." I have always tried to steward people's tithes and offerings thoughtfully, because I know that sometimes people are out of work or living on the bottom line or hungry, and they're still tithing. Because it's God's money, I have never thought, *Wow, we have a $10-million budget! Let's go buy stuff.* But I did think like this: "Lord, please don't let me lose millions that people trusted us with."

I didn't tell the church about the problem, but I walked with God and had long talks with Him about it. Some Water of Life members probably walked by me in the hallways during this time and thought, *Wow, you're not very friendly*. The truth is, I just don't talk to people when stuff like this happens, except my wife and maybe the guys on the board. I go to God about stuff like this, because that's where I've learned to go. This is what God wants us to do, because He is always able. He's greater than our situations, and He longs for us to run to Him and trust Him.

We have to keep believing and keep pressing into God, no matter how difficult life gets.

In June 2012, we renegotiated our contract with the owner and partner of the Sierra property. They required another immediate payment of $1.5 million, which we were able to pay through the generosity of those who had given to the Until the Whole World Hears campaign and during the Blessed Life teaching series and also from the Water of Life Christian School fund. This would bring our paid amount up to $3 million. Then they came up with a new payment deadline of January 15, 2013, for the final $2 million. This was a hard deadline, and everyone knew it.

I came back to the church and told the people, "We extended to January 15, but I think we're going to pay the land off by December."

What happened in the next six months was beyond phenomenal—it was supernatural and miraculous. From June to December, God opened up heaven in people's hearts, and some who had never tithed, never given, never understood worship this way before, began giving. Suddenly our general giving shot up.

By December we had raised the final $2 million that we owed, and we paid off the Sierra property in December 2012. *Thank You, God!*

But here's the amazing thing: In January 2013, as our numbers man Mark Bluethman was looking back at Water of Life's giving amounts from the previous two years, he noticed something very interesting. In 2011 our general and building-fund giving combined had been $7.1 million. In 2012 it was $10.8

million—a surprising increase. But an increase of how much? It was $3.7 million—exactly the amount we had been short at the beginning of 2012, when I had been persistently laying the matter before God.

Now you may think that was a coincidence. But in 2012 we needed $3.7 million, and God gave it to us. When we started pushing the buttons on the calculator and this number came up, we were more shocked than anyone. This was not an accident. This was a miracle, especially in that economy. In the last six months of our need, God made a way when there was no way. How generous He was to us!

But note this: that same year we gave away over a million dollars to bless the poor and also a number of missionaries. We gave to Living Word Ministries in Thailand to support orphanages, a new crisis pregnancy center in Fontana, WOW JAMS, River's Edge Men's Ranch, Pastor Friday in Nigeria for a school that his ministry was building, Bengali Evangelistic Association in Bangladesh, King's University, outreaches in Cambodia, and Agua de Vida orphanage, just to name a few.

As we blessed people, God blessed us. As we were faithful, God was faithful to us.

Please don't miss the faith factor of the people of Water of Life in all this. God uses people, and many people sacrificed in huge ways to help us pay off the Sierra property. They believed in what God was doing at Water of Life and in their own lives. God's still moving, is He not? He's very alive.

I hope this story helps you to believe in a bigger way. Had the Sierra property gone into foreclosure and had I lost my job, I still wouldn't have given up on God. There's nowhere else to go but to Him. We must settle it in our minds and in our hearts—our hope is in God. We have to keep believing and keep pressing into Him, no matter how difficult life gets. He is our refuge and our ever-present help in the time of need.

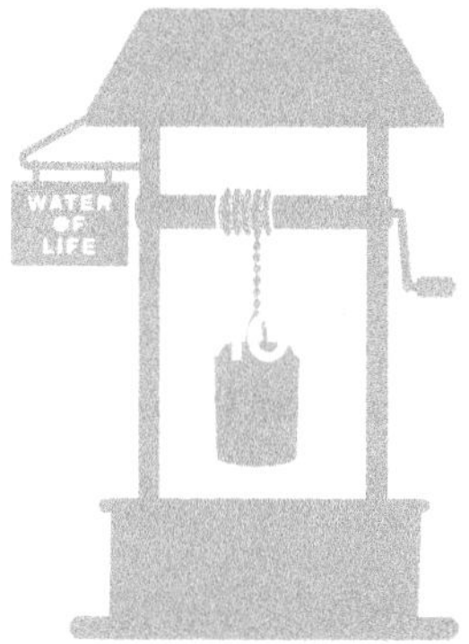

God's Multiplication

2013–2015

God can multiply things. The problem is, we think that God doesn't really want to give back to us what we give up for Him. But He does. In fact, God doesn't just give back what we give up—He gives back more.

Water of Life had been the owners of the land on Sierra for only a few weeks when we got a phone call from a real estate agent who asked if we wanted to sell the property. He offered us $14 million.

No way we're going to sell, we thought. *God just gave us this property*.

The next week another guy called and said, "Did you guys just buy that property for an investment? If you did, you really bought it at the right time. We're willing to offer you at least $17 million for it right now."

That's a lot of money, I thought. *But it's just money. It's not destiny*. I never think in terms of money. Instead I think, *God, what are You saying?* Land and buildings are never the story. Faith is always the story. And people are the story.

But God uses land and buildings to build faith and to touch people, and God wanted Water of Life to touch more people in bigger ways, so we paid attention. We wondered what God was doing.

The offers on the Sierra property kept coming in and climbing, finally reaching $24 million. At about $20 million the elders decided to stop and pray and see what this was all about. Maybe the Lord was doing something that we hadn't foreseen.

I also called Jack Hayford and Robert Morris for advice. "We've been getting offers for $14 million, $17 million, now $24 million," I told them.

Pastor Jack said, "I would sell the land and build on your own property. Do you have room to do that?" It wasn't an ideal plan, as we'd seen in 2008 when we had first looked into it, but we would be able to pay a huge amount of the costs without financing if we sold the Sierra property and used the proceeds to build on East Avenue.

Pastor Robert felt that he had a word from the Lord for us. "I think that the Lord is blessing you," he told me, "and that you're supposed to sell."

The elders realized that perhaps the land on Sierra had not been for us to build on but rather God's provision for us to build at East Avenue and be good stewards of our resources and debt load. We even reached out to the guy who had sold us the property—after all, he had bought it for $17 million and then sold it to us for $5 million. Now we wanted to turn around and sell it for $24 million. That was kind of painful for someone in his shoes. But he was okay with us selling it.

After prayer and discussion, we decided to sell the Sierra property—and build a new worship center on East Avenue. What a turn of events! But it was very clearly God's answer to the problem we'd struggled with for years.

The Sierra property quickly went into escrow at $24 million with a home developer, which the city planning commission initially approved. But when the matter went to a public vote, the property was rezoned to commercial, so we lost the sale. Talk about ups and downs.

City council members came to me and told me how sorry they were. I simply told them, "My hope is not in the city—it's in the Lord. He will work it out." Within weeks a group of warehousing developers contacted us and wanted to buy the land. By March 2013, we were in escrow again—this time for $20.5 million.

We wanted to move quickly on our plans to build on East Avenue, using the same basic blueprints that we had drawn up in 2008. But what about the parking and traffic flow issues that had stopped us the first time around?

Well, God had actually worked out the details for us in the last few years. As with any church or business, we paid taxes, some of which went to the city of Fontana. Several years after we moved to East Avenue, one of our accountants had discovered that we had been billed for and had paid what is called a Mello-Roos tax. Mello-Roos funds are used by local municipalities to pay for infrastructure improvements—roads and sidewalks and such. As a non-profit, we were not required to pay this tax.

We approached city hall, and officials there agreed that we had been improperly taxed. We were owed a refund. The officials asked us to file a friendly lawsuit against the city so that a judge could determine the outcome. So we went to court, and a judge ruled that we were owed $300,000. The city didn't have that much in its budget, so they offered us an alternative: did we want the city to give us the land under the Edison utility towers that stretches from East Avenue to Baseline—almost next door to the church?

Of course we wanted the narrow strip of land. Instantly our parking problem was solved! Well, not quite so instantly—we had to do some negotiating with Edison—but once the details were hammered out, we had enough space for parking. Without these lots, we could not have moved forward with our new building. Another miracle to add to the list.

We tweaked our former building plans a bit, and in August 2013, we started an aggressive building initiative. For the new project, we would (1) renovate the single-story building to maximize space for the Christian school and for our kids' programs; (2) move our administrative offices from the two-story building to a separate building a few miles away on Miller Avenue and move the kids' classrooms temporarily into the two-story building; (3) add two new parking lots on Liberty Parkway (more of the property given us by the city of Fontana!) and create a bridge and access road to Baseline Avenue; (4) build a 3,500-square-foot storage building to house equipment and supplies as well as offices, workshop areas, and bays for our facilities staff; (5) build a parking garage where the south parking lot was; and (6), most obviously, build a worship center that would seat three thousand people and would include a prayer tower, a coffee shop, a bookstore, and multiple classrooms and offices.

When all the numbers were crunched—building costs, permits, etc.—the project estimate totaled $35 million. Whoa. The sale of the Sierra property would help us a lot, but we still had to raise some funds.

Shortly before we started the Pressing In Because People Matter campaign, God started to speak to Gale and me about it. I've read my Bible, and I know that Chronicles 28 says that leaders are supposed to lead. When I prayed about the building costs, God said to me, "Yeah, I want you to lead."

Oh, boy. I knew what that meant. I buy and sell real estate sometimes, particularly to earn some income to put away for retirement. I'd saved some money, and I was planning to use $35,000 of my savings to buy a certain house. I also wanted to help my kids pay off some of their school bills to the tune of about $60,000 each.

But God was really clear with me. He said, "I want you to give up the money."

Half jokingly I told the Lord, "That's a super bad strategy."

The Lord didn't let me off the hook. "I know you don't like My strategy, but just give up the money."

So I did. On the last day of December 2013, Gale and I wrote a check for the amount of our entire savings, and we gave it to the building fund. I did it willingly, not begrudgingly, but I did ask God, "Now, God, how are You going to pay for the kids' school?"

A few weeks after we wrote that check, we found out that we were going to get $14,000 back on our taxes. Then a few days after that, I got an e-mail telling me that an investment that Gale and I had made had earned $15,000. All I could say was, "Thank You, God." When God tells us to give, He gives back to us.

**God was really clear with me.
He said, "I want you to give up the money."**

Our leadership interviewed several general contractors and selected Pacific Providence. That company had done numerous projects for churches, including some for Chuck Smith and the Calvary Chapel movement. It was an added bonus to discover that the owners were committed Christians.

On January 26, 2014, we had our groundbreaking ceremony for the new worship center on East Avenue in what was formerly our gravel parking lot. This was a special time of worship, prayer, and praise.

In February we launched our Pressing In Because People Matter campaign, and on commitment Sunday, April 13, 2014, people pledged $16,556,871—more than had ever been committed in a Water of Life campaign before.

We spent 2014 and most of 2015 encouraging people to work with what we called our Shift initiative, helping them figure out where to park in our offsite lots and ride the shuttle buses in for church. It was hard to get to church, but people were excited to watch as the single story was renovated, as the south parking lot on the main East Avenue site was torn up to make way for the parking garage, and as the huge building with its prayer tower slowly took shape.

The construction of this building was the result of many, many years of praying and believing, and now we were watching those prayers being answered. Prayer and faith were the foundation and the catalyst for the new worship center, and they would continue to be our strength.

At the groundbreaking ceremony and throughout the year, we had given out cards and asked people to write down their prayers regarding the new building. Who would they reach? Who would they touch? Whose lives did they hope would be changed forever? On January 10, 2015, at ten in the morning, hundreds and hundreds of the written prayers that people were believing God to fulfill in the new worship center were ceremoniously laid into the foundation as a symbol of our trust that prayers would be answered and lives touched through the ministry that would take place inside the walls of the new worship center.

In February 2015, we met with the fire department and Fontana city officials to ask an important question: would we be able to hold our upcoming Easter services in our incomplete worship center? Initially they had many objections, but by the end of the meeting, all the objections were overcome, and they gave their approval.

On the weekend of April 3–5, 2015, almost exactly fifteen years after we first moved onto the East Avenue property, we held our Good Friday and Easter services in the new partially finished worship center. We had an amazing time of celebration and thanksgiving. That weekend, in our soft opening of the new sanctuary, about twelve hundred people came forward to the altar. As people streamed forward, some of them weeping, I was moved to tears. "This," I told the people gathered, pointing to the crowds at the altar, "is what this building is all about."

The escrow with Sierra proved to be long and drawn out and full of complications and delays. But finally, after nearly fifteen months in escrow, we completed the final thirty-day waiting period, and the bank started the process to close the property. On Tuesday, April 14, 2015, the loan was funded and recorded, and a check for $20.5 million was transferred into our bank account.

God is into multiplication. When God first spoke with Abraham, He said, "I want to multiply you," which means, "I want to exponentially expand you. I want to do something in you so great that it will expand to other people."

Back in 2010, after everybody had been laid off work and things were bad, I was saying to people, "I know you don't have any money, but believe God to do something bigger than you, to touch people you know and people you don't know in ways that you can't imagine. Give your money to buy this piece of land on Sierra."

It wasn't easy for people to give back then. But people were faithful. One lady wrote to me,

> Pastor Dan, I am a widow. My husband died three years ago. I didn't have any idea how I could survive. But God has sustained me in so many ways.
>
> I had been trying to sell our RV for two years, and *no one was interested*. This was really hard for me, because I had to pay the storage fee on it every month, and I was never using it. When I decided to make a commitment to "Pressing in—Because People Matter" and help build the building, I wrote out my commitment card for the building, and I committed $3,000. I told God, "You sell the RV, I'll give the money." But the RV hadn't sold for two years. No worries. Because now it was in all in God's hands to sell it.
>
> Well, this is the truth: after I signed the card, I got so many calls on the RV. It was as if everybody wanted it now because it had the favor of God on it. I sold it. I paid my $3,000 commitment, and I just want to encourage people,

if you give what you can, God will give the rest. Praise God every day because He loves me so much.

That is faith. Those people who gave to the Until the Whole World Hears campaign believed for people they couldn't even see and bought the land on Sierra, and God turned their $5 million into $20.5 million for our new worship center here on East Avenue. That's called multiplication.

Another couple, Mark and Marcia, had made a pledge to the Pressing In campaign and felt good about their decision, but then one Sunday I preached about giving a larger amount of money. They had just sold their house and had a little bit of extra money. Marcia shared with the Water of Life staff, "We both felt convicted that we should give some of that, but I really struggled because I selfishly wanted that money to fix up our new house. I had quite a few discussions with God about it, but as I had time alone with God and felt like we were supposed to do it, Mark and I found out that we had each come up with the exact same amount in prayer that we thought God wanted us to give. What an awesome peace came over us.

"To stand in the new church on Easter Sunday and listen to the music and realize that you're part of that is just the biggest blessing," Marcia continued. "I just couldn't stop tearing up the whole weekend because we're part of that, and that's just amazing."

Her husband, Mark, added, "The whole Easter experience was just awesome. It's great to build a building, but it's changing lives that is really the big thing. We saw that on Easter. We're going to continue to press in. Whether it's for the building or whatever God wants to do with the church, we're in."

That's exactly right. It's not about buildings—it's about people. The investment that people have made over the years—from the money in the cocoa can to the Inherit the Land campaign to the campaigns to buy the land on Sierra and then to build on East Avenue—hasn't just resulted in multiplied funds. It has resulted in multiplied lives. That's what we saw on Easter in the new worship center when twelve hundred people came forward to the altar.

The word "faithfulness" means "full of faith." All those people who came forward, all those people who got touched on Easter—they were touched because of people who were faithful back in 2010. The people who gave back then couldn't see any of these people who would come in 2015, but they said, "We're going to believe anyway." Remember, faith is the assurance of something that we hope for, and people were hoping for those lives. Faith is also the conviction of things that we can't see, and those people were sure of something that they couldn't see.

Easter weekend rocked our world. But something else rocked too: people at Water of Life who believed for people they would never see. These people said, "I'm going to sacrifice. I'm going to give. I'm going to surrender myself. I'm going to let God have His way in my life," even when others around them thought that they were crazy.

During this season, when I was taking a week-long class at King's Seminary, I was talking to Jack Hayford about Water of Life and our building program. I didn't tell him that we needed money or how big the project was, only that it was pressing me. Before I left that week, Pastor Jack wrote me a personal check made out to Water of Life Community Church for $10,000, and he said, "I want to make a difference in the people of your church. I am in this battle with you."

Pastor Jack has made a huge impact on me. I learned that day not just to be a sacrificial giver but that giving is warfare. It is part of spiritual warfare, because it is a dangerous threat to the enemy. You and I and all of us who are part of the body of Christ are in a battle for the hearts of men and women and children.

Years ago God told me, "I'm going to change the world through your hooking up your little ladybug trailer on your Malibu car." I didn't feel like doing it. But I had faithful people around me. I wouldn't be here today if I hadn't had faithful friends around me like Pastor Rolo, who was always saying, "No, don't leave. Stay. God can do it." And remember my two kids who hated setting up chairs at La Petite childcare center? Today my son, Shane, is on staff at Water of Life, directing our young adult ministries and our global outreach, and my daughter, Katie, is a nurse practitioner planning on moving soon to Cambodia, where she will train nurses to care for the poor. God multiplied what we put in.

On August 9, 2015, Water of Life celebrated our twenty-five-year anniversary at Glen Helen Regional Park. Andy Taylor and our amazing worship team led us in a time of praise and worship—we had come a long way since Jeff Krausman and the Cassettes! Jeremy Camp followed with a concert, celebrating with us twenty-five years of believing, praying, giving, sacrificing, and waiting on God as He led us along a path that we couldn't see in advance. Brian Snowball, who has been such a vital part of our maintenance team and our building projects, summed it up well: "The journey continues—it just keeps getting bigger and bigger. And I think, *Wow, this must be what the kingdom's gonna be like.*"

Two months before the completion of the new worship center, church leaders met with the architect, and we were talking about the furniture needed for the fourteen one- and two-year-old classrooms in the new building. I wondered what kind of furniture we needed for one- and two-year-olds. Don't you just put them on the floor? Okay, I know, they need changing tables and rocking chairs. How much was this going to cost? The price tag was $88,000.

I looked at the architect and asked, "How much is in the budget for this?"

"The budget's gone, Pastor," he told me.

I took the need to the church and asked them to pray. That very day a family came up to me and gave me $5,000 to help fill the need. Now that was a great gift, but it was only the beginning, because the next day I got an e-mail from a man who wanted to give $50,000 for the classroom furniture. He also wrote that if we didn't have all the money by the end of week, I should give him a call.

I didn't need to call him. By the grace of God, he went ahead and increased the amount of his check to $75,000. God is constantly multiplying back to Water of Life what our people have given to Him, and He will multiply back to these individuals as well.

The journey continues—it just keeps getting bigger and bigger. This must be what the kingdom of God is going to be like.

On Sunday, November 15, 2015, we will celebrate the opening of our new worship center with Jack and Anna Hayford and many of those who helped along the way. The journey to this place has been a remarkable one, full of mountains and valleys. So often God cul-de-sacs us, and we want to turn on Him, but He is testing us. That was the whole journey of Israel—God closed them up to see what they would do. Water of Life has certainly been tested, but as a church we have stayed in with God, and we are reaping and will continue to reap the rewards of God's multiplication.

It's not an accident that Water of Life is on East Avenue—it's our destiny. We embrace it. We keep praying for the church to touch neighborhoods and nations—and to touch people. We are believing the Holy Spirit to move people to keep giving, serving, and pressing in, and we are believing God to build His kingdom and transform people's lives. Our story of faith has been wild so far, but there is still more to come . . .

Afterword

Faith that God Marvels At

God loves memorials. He wants to make you a memorial. God wants to use you so that someday people will say, "Those people changed me."

But that takes faith. Twenty-one people started this church, and they believed God for your life. They never saw you, they never knew you, but they believed for you. The 275 people who prayed over this property when we first made an offer on it believed for you. The hundreds of people who gave money to buy the land on Sierra and later to build our new worship center here on East Avenue believed for you. Their faith has impacted people's lives and destinies. Every one of those people is a memorial.

God wants to make you a memorial. For Him to do that, you have to believe that the decisions you make today will impact thousands and thousands of people you're never going to see.

There's a story in Luke 7 about a Roman centurion who believed God for a miracle:

> A centurion's slave, who was highly regarded by him, was sick and about to die. When he heard about Jesus, he sent some Jewish elders asking Him to come and save the life of his slave. When they came to Jesus, they earnestly implored Him, saying, "He is worthy for You to grant this to him; for he loves our nation and it was he who built us our synagogue." Now Jesus started on His way with them; and when He was not far from the house, the centurion sent friends, saying to Him, "Lord, do not trouble Yourself further, for I am not worthy for You to come under my roof; for this reason I did not even consider myself worthy to come to You, but just say the word, and my servant will be healed. For I also am a man placed under authority, with soldiers under me; and I say to this one, 'Go!' and he goes, and to another, 'Come!' and he comes, and to my slave, 'Do this!' and he does it." Now when Jesus heard this, He marveled at him, and turned and said to the crowd that was following Him, "I say to you, not even in Israel have I found such great faith." When those who had been sent returned to the house, they found the slave in good health. (Luke 7:2–10)

"Just say the word," this guy said, and Jesus was like, "Whoa, dude, where did you get that kind of faith? You did not find that in Rome. In fact, you probably didn't even get that in Israel, because even My people don't believe like that. Where did your faith come from?"

You know what is interesting? Jesus Christ put that faith in that man. And listen, He's trying to download faith inside you right now. When you receive it, like this man did, Jesus will just marvel at you: "Look at you go. Whoo-hoo, go, girl. Look at you, man. I can't believe that you would trust Me when you can't see what I'm doing. It's out in the future, but you believe Me anyway."

This Roman centurion is an amazing person in the Bible, because it says in Luke that Jesus marveled at his faith. That word "marveled" is used only twice in the New Testament. Once here and on one other occasion when Jesus marveled about some people's lack of faith.

In Mark 6, when Jesus was in Nazareth, His hometown, and tried to heal people, the people had such a lack of faith that He couldn't heal anybody. He had grown up there, and none of the people believed that He was Messiah. They all looked at Him and said, "Dude, we used to skateboard with You. You cannot be the Messiah." And Jesus marveled at their lack of faith, at their unbelief, because He wanted so badly to help them, and they wouldn't let Him.

But the Roman centurion—Jesus marveled at his faith because it was so high.

Let me ask you a question: do you want God to marvel at your faith? Here's a bigger question: how do you want Him to marvel at your faith? Do you want Him to marvel at your unbelief or at your belief?

Too often God marvels at our unbelief. We come to church, we listen, we read the Word, we worship, but we don't believe God. When the rubber meets the road, we don't believe God. But the Roman centurion's faith was absolute and unlimited: "Just say the word, and I know that You will heal my servant, even from a distance." Do you want faith like that? I do. I want to say, "God, I know that things look bad. This journey is tough, and it hurts, and I don't know where You're taking me. But I know that You've got this."

How do we get that kind of faith? This guy gives us the answer right there in verses 7–8. He says, "Just say the word, and my servant will be healed. For I also am a man placed under authority, with soldiers under me; and I say to this one, 'Go!' and he goes, and to another, 'Come!' and he comes, and to my slave, 'Do this!' and he does it." How did this guy know that Jesus could heal? Because he was "under authority."

Please figure this out. Around here I tell you to get on your number and stay there. When I was a P.E. teacher, every kid in my

P.E. classes had a number. I would blow the whistle and say, "Get your big head on your number, because I'm going to take roll now, and I need you to be on your number." If your name was Applebee, you were number one. If your name was Zimmermann, you were number 163.

Too often we don't want to be on our own number; we want to be somewhere else. But if we would just listen to the guy's answer, "I am a man under authority"—that's where his faith came from, right there. He submitted himself to a living God, and God blew up his world—He changed his life, healed his servant, and healed his heart.

If you want God to make you a memorial, if you want God to use you to change other people's lives, if you want God to marvel at your great faith, then find out what your number is, and get on it. And stay on it. God will use you, and He will multiply back to you everything you give to Him.

About the Author

Dan Carroll grew up in Pomona, California. In February 1970, he received Christ as his savior at a Youth for Christ meeting. In 1976 he received a B.A. in religion from the University of La Verne and went on to teach in the Pomona Unified School District for three years. Then in 1979 he received his M.A. in education from the Claremont Graduate University. Dan and his wife moved to Idaho, where he taught high-school English and history and coached the basketball team. He also served as an elder at Community Fellowship Church.

In 1982 Dan took a youth-pastor position at Life Bible Fellowship in Upland, California, and served there until 1987. He received an M.A. in Christian Ministry from the International School of Theology in 1987.

In 1987 Pastor Dan began teaching a men's Bible study. For three years the study grew in scope and depth, and the families of the men involved began to come together for fellowship. In 1989 Dan and his family went to the Youth With A Mission training school in Kona, Hawaii. They were introduced to cross-cultural ministry in Penang, Malaysia, where Dan received a vision for the world. After returning to the United States in 1990, he was encouraged by the men of his Bible study and their families to plant a church. This became Water of Life Community Church.

Pastor Dan completed a doctorate of ministry from the King's Seminary in 2004. He continues today as the senior pastor of Water of Life Community Church.

Dan and Gale have been married for thirty-seven years and have two adult children, Shane and Katie.

About Water of Life

Water of Life Community Church is a non-denominational evangelical charismatic church. This means that we are devoted to studying and obeying the Bible, which is the Word of God, and that we believe in the baptism of the Holy Spirit and the modern-day operation of the gifts proclaimed in the New Testament.

Water of Life was established on Sunday, October 28, 1990, when a group of twenty-one adults and eleven children gathered together to worship at the La Petite childcare building in Rancho Cucamonga, California. It was a fellowship that arose from a men's Bible study, a group of people who grew together, and a body that is now committed together to seek God's plan as a church family.

Many people love God but have become disillusioned with the church. Therefore, a church that offers a personal encounter with Jesus Christ and growth in His Word without the clutter of an overly structured environment has great appeal. Because we want to maintain the integrity and purity of our spiritual purpose, we do not have a rigorous structure with multitudes of committees or membership requirements.

Our desire is to walk by faith and in deep trust of our Lord. Consequently, you will not see us take an offering. Rather, we believe that the giving of tithes and offerings is worship to Jesus Christ and an expression of the relationship between each individual giver and the Lord.

Although Water of Life is a non-denominational church, we consider ourselves a church that is interdependent with the rest of the body of Christ. Our church is governed by our pastors and our elder board. Additionally, our senior pastor is accountable to an outside group of senior pastors from other local churches as well as to an internationally recognized leader from the Foursquare denomination.

Our Core Values

Healing

Healing is the very starting point of a transformed life. It speaks to maturing people into a closer relationship with Christ, not just to getting better inside. Jesus put a huge value on healing—putting people back together again. Healing of sick, wounded, and broken lives is a high priority to a compassionate and loving God:

> The Spirit of the LORD is upon me, for he has anointed me to bring Good News to the poor. He has sent me to proclaim that captives will be released, that the blind will see, that the oppressed will be set free, and that the time of the LORD's favor has come. (Luke 4:18–19, NLT)

Healing is so important to God that He made it a key part of discipleship, or growing in Jesus. Healing occurred many times in Jesus' ministry, and miracles frequently occurred. But Jesus' healing was not just about making people well physically. Rather, it was to restore them in the kingdom of God, to bring them into a right relationship with God. Ephesians 4:11–13 talks of apostles, prophets, evangelists, pastors, and teachers all having the responsibility "to equip God's people to do his work and build up the church, the body of Christ. . . until we all come to such unity in our faith and knowledge of God's Son that we will be mature in the Lord, measuring up to the full and complete standard of Christ" (4:12–13, NLT). The word "equip," *kartatizo* in Greek, means "to mend, restore and be put back together."

> I will sprinkle clean water on you, and you will be clean. Your filth will be washed away, and you will no longer worship idols. And I will give you a new heart, and I will put a new spirit in you. I will take out your stony, stubborn heart and give you a tender, responsive heart. And I will put my Spirit in you so you will follow my decrees and be careful to obey my regulations. (Ezek. 36:25–27, NLT)

The goal in all we do must be transformation—that is where winning begins. God has called us into relationship with one another so that we can be healed and then become instruments of His healing.

> Blessed be the God and Father of our Lord Jesus Christ, the Father of mercies and God of all comfort, who comforts us in all our affliction so that we will be able to comfort those who are in any affliction with the comfort with which we ourselves are comforted by God. (2 Cor. 1:3–4)

God does not call us to store up what He gives us but to pass it on to others. Transformation occurs in our church's small groups as well as in our healing and recovery groups, in which people can find support, care, prayer, and encouragement.

Sending

Sending is our second core value. We believe it is foundational to all that God wants to do in us.

Everything about us likes to be comfortable, but Jesus told us that the way for us to grow is to be stretched out (*ekteno* in the Greek). We need to get out of our comfort zones.

In Acts 13:1–3 we read that the church in Jerusalem sent Paul and Barnabas out on the first real missionary journey. Their goal was to reproduce the work God had done in them and in other believers by spreading the word of Jesus' love and transforming lives and starting churches. This church-planting model has been followed in various forms ever since. Our desire at Water of Life is to send teams out for short-term exposure on a regular basis and at the same time to train and expose our church to as many cross-cultural types of ministry as possible. This includes those near to us (in our valley) and those far from us (all over the world). In our history we have sent short-term teams to between fifteen and twenty different countries, including Malaysia, Hong Kong, Russia, China, Jamaica, Venezuela, Guatemala, Lebanon, Panama, Kenya, Nicaragua, El Salvador, Cuba, and Honduras. More recently, we have sent teams to Mexico, Cambodia, and Thailand.

Jesus told His disciples in Matthew 28:19, "Go therefore and make disciples of all the nations, baptizing them in the name of the Father and the Son and the Holy Spirit." In Acts 1:4–8 He told them more:

> Gathering them together, He commanded them not to leave Jerusalem, but to wait for what the Father had promised, "Which," He said, "you heard of from Me; for John baptized with water, but you will be baptized with the Holy Spirit not many days from now." So when they had come together, they were asking Him, saying, "Lord, is it at this time You are restoring the kingdom to Israel?" He said to them, "It is not for you to know times or epochs which the

> Father has fixed by His own authority; but you will receive power when the Holy Spirit has come upon you; and you shall be My witnesses both in Jerusalem, and in all Judea and Samaria, and even to the remotest part of the earth.

Jerusalem and Judea were home to Jesus and the disciples—that is, local. So we likewise do local outreach at our food-and-clothing warehouse, with our mobile medical unit, and with our annual Trunk-or-Treat Halloween-alternative event. The remote parts of the world for Water of Life are Cambodia and Thailand as well as other nations we have reached. This outreach is all based on Holy Spirit empowerment, and we seek to establish long-term relationships in each of these areas. This will result in transformed lives—in us as we go and in others as they receive.

Equipping

> And He gave some as apostles, and some as prophets, and some as evangelists, and some as pastors and teachers, for the equipping of the saints for the work of service, to the building up of the body of Christ. (Eph. 4:11–12)

This core value, like the ones before it, speaks to transforming lives. At Water of Life winning is defined as "a transformed life demonstrated by a person being given to God and given to other people." In regard to equipping, as we at Water of Life learn the truth in the Word of God, we receive training along with it as to what we are to do with what we learn. Following God is not just about words—it is an action. A changed person is one who loves God and loves people as well as serves God and serves people.

Equipping at Water of Life means more than just attending church or a Bible study: "The things which you have heard from me in the presence of many witnesses, entrust these to faithful men who will be able to teach others also" (2 Tim. 2:2).

At Water of Life, equipping means teaching and releasing people with the purpose of both mind transformation and heart transformation. Practically speaking, all our small groups will teach and do outreach ministry in which they extend themselves to others. Individuals as well are provided with the opportunity to serve by caring for others—putting their knowledge to work to give life to other people.

Caring

> What use is it, my brethren, if someone says he has faith but has no works? Can that faith save him? If a brother or sister is without clothing and in need of daily food, and one of you says to them, "Go in peace, be warmed and be filled," and yet you do not give them what is necessary for their body, what use is that? Even so faith, if it has no works, is dead, being by itself. (James 2:14–17)

We believe that one of Water of Life's main priorities is to care for those in need. The principle is this: we get so we can give. We believe this is a part of God's heart for all people. We need the poor and downtrodden as much as they need us. It is through them that we gain the heart of God and the Holy Spirit is able to soften us and impart the Father's heart to us.

The Bible is emphatic about the church's responsibility to care for those in need: "But whoever has the world's goods, and sees his brother [or sister] in need and closes his heart against him, how does the love of God abide in him?" (1 John 3:17).

In Matthew 25 we read that Jesus expects nothing less from His church, which is why this core value is so important at Water of Life.

This expectation is clearly shown in Scripture:

> Then the King will say to those on His right, "Come, you who are blessed of My Father, inherit the kingdom prepared for you from the foundation of the world. For I was hungry, and you gave Me something to eat; I was thirsty, and you gave Me something to drink; I was a stranger, and you invited Me in; naked, and you clothed Me; I was sick, and you visited Me; I was in prison, and you came to Me." (Matt. 25:34–36)

We want to be counted among the faithful described above as those who fed the hungry, gave drink to the thirsty, invited the stranger in, clothed the naked, cared for the sick, and also visited those in prison. "The King will answer and say to them, 'Truly I say to you, to the extent that you did it to one of these brothers of Mine, even the least of them, you did it to Me" (Matt. 25:40).

Relationships

Lives are transformed through relationships—community and family relationships: "You are citizens along with all of God's holy people. You are members of God's family. . . . We [who believe] are carefully joined together in him, becoming a holy temple for the Lord" (Eph. 2:19, 21, NLT).

Everyone who believes in Jesus is part of His family. He has joined us together, and He tells us that we should get along. He is the One who holds everything together. He holds the world together, He holds marriages together, He holds the church family together, and He holds personal relationships together: "He is before all things, and in Him all things hold together" (Col. 1:17).

First Corinthians is quite clear in telling us that He put all of us together; we are one body, and we are supposed to live as if we are:

> For even as the body is one and yet has many members, and all the members of the body, though they are many,

> are one body, so also is Christ. For by one Spirit we were all baptized into one body, whether Jews or Greeks, whether slaves or free, and we were all made to drink of one Spirit. (1 Cor. 12:12–13)

The rules of the family of God are clear and simple: we are called to serve one another. This is only possible through our relationship with Jesus. To have a powerful and on-fire relationship with Jesus, we have to get our mind off ourselves and choose to focus on other people. Christ always did this. He built His relationships with many people based on compassion, and He asks us to do the same. In Mark 1:41, as Jesus spoke with a leper, He was "moved with compassion." He stretched out His hand, touched the leper and healed him. In order for us to be really connected with others at a deep level, we must be compassionate.

The heart of a servant is a heart of compassion. There is power in serving others, and there is also blessing in serving others. As we come together in right relationship with other people, we position ourselves to be blessed by God.

Contact us at:

Water of Life Community Church
7625 East Avenue, Fontana, CA, 92336

Water of Life Administration Office
14418 Miller Avenue, Suite K, Fontana, CA 92336
Phone: 909.463.0103
Fax: 909.463.1436
E-mail: info@wateroflifecc.org